Lucie

All inquiries are welcome:

Judy Block
Friday in France
502 Raehn Street
Orlando, FL 32806
JUDYBLOCK@BELLSOUTH.NET

ISBN-13: 978-0692567166 (Custom)
ISBN-10: 069256716X

Author's note: The events described in this book are primarily true. Certain dates or details have been slightly adjusted for the sake of the story-arc and clarity.

Videota
Library of Congress Copyright Registration #1-213301111
Friday in France, Author and publisher, Judy Block 2ND~ed.

FRIDAY IN FRANCE

Friday in France

CONTENTS

Friday in France

Chapter 1: The Upper West Side

Life is either a daring adventure or nothing.
~ Helen Keller

New York City, January 1993

"Two minutes to air," the shrill sound falls out my mouth, it's an automatic response. My voice reverberates and bounces back-off the walls of the small edit room. Meanwhile the editor is focused on the last few cuts and never takes his hands off of the equipment.

He mumbles, "You'll have it," keeping his mind wrapped-around the task at hand. My hands are wrapped tightly around the receiver of the studio-hotline as if holding on tighter will some-how keep me grounded. The death grip I have makes my hands sweaty. Squeezing the phone gives me the illusion of feeling closer and more connected to the entire show unit down the hall in the control room of Studio A. I keep a keen eye on the clock. I look at my clipboard with a show- rundown that seems to glare back at me; it mocks me with the obviously absent elements to a show that is already on the air... LIVE.

A rash of vile language spews directly into my ear, an assault from the control room's Associate Producer; her stress is a reasonable reaction. I'm irritated though, doing my best and act as if I'm (almost) confident in my words, "You'll have the story, you'll have it," I said... "You'll have it!"

I cover the phone, "Under a minute—let's go." The edit room energy goes from a measurable buzz to a full-tilt frenzy, the tension pings around the tiny edit room. Instinctively and automatically I slip out of my fabulous Italian-black leather pumps – I ready myself.

The editor punches the keys on the record deck with a directness that makes him seem angry. He's not. He's skilled, he's alert and he is doing his best to block me out. His pace ramps up to a feverish pitch and the key pad takes a final beating. Now with one more move the machine works to mechanically cue the tape up to the top of the piece; my job's quite simple actually... stand-still, wait and remember to inhale. My heart is pounding and feels like it has made its way to my throat or in my hand or wherever it isn't supposed to be... and yet this is so typical every night at 6 o'clock, 6:02, 6:03, 6:04 etc. Despite the nightly routine of pushing deadlines I always feel the intense anxiety and powerful rush of adrenaline. The strain and trauma of working in live news... each one of these moments has a weight of its own. Twenty of these moments a day begins to eat away at your spirit (my spirit). And yet- somewhere along the way, perhaps after years and years of the same thing... it becomes the norm.

Forty-three seconds to air and he reaches for the eject button and we wait for it to react. His hand acts like a greedy catchers-mitt waiting at the bottom of the ninth. In the eight long (insanely long) seconds the machine takes to lift the tape off of the machine's playback heads, I yell into the phone, "On my way..." I hang up and put my hand out into mid-air as I simultaneously and seamlessly use my butt to push open the edit room door. One swift movement, a habitual response I've lived over and over again.

He slams the tape into my hand with a forceful move... I begin to make the mad-dash down the hall; from zero to 60 mph in- less than two seconds. The sprint is an all important part of my job; it always seems like a matter of life or death. Truly it's a matter of making air or not which is a big enough motivator for me to move my sorry-ass as fast as possible. I race toward the general direction of the playback operator and throw the tape into his hands. I never really stop as I round the bend, past the record decks, the satellite desk- operators and countless, reasonably uninterested, onlookers. Twenty-two seconds to air and I slide my way into the control-room; my black-stockings assisting me in this slippery move.

I look towards the AP and yell, "Total running time, one minute, fifty-two seconds, out-cue for NBC News." At the exact same time I hear the anchor on-air read the very last line of the story intro and I take a deep breath. I silently pray that the playback operator has it cued up correctly. The tape rolls seamlessly on-air as if it's been parked there for hours. I give a knowing glance around the room to the execs on the back-deck. The *'I told you we'd make air'* is silently implied, then I push the control room door open. I work my way back to the videotape department to find my clipboard.

As I saunter down the hall, I start to do the math in my mind-- I'm all too aware that the entire back half of this show is still missing; it's mine to deal with and I think of how to pace myself. I make my plan with highlighted notes-this helps to reassure and soothe and somehow distract myself from the knot growing in my stomach.

My heart happily begins to beat back in its rightful place. I walk past my desk on my way to edit room four, where the next reporter, producer, editor and piece of missing tape are located. I know I have at least two minutes and twenty seconds to spare. I take the time to grab a few Tums and chomp on them. The heartburn won't go away, but it's a ritual of sorts, one that I'm not sure yet if I know how to let go of.

The rest of my desk is oddly empty... it actually looks clean for the first time in years. It reminds me that this will be my last night of running tapes down the hall. This will be my last night of testing my heart-rate. The last night that I'll be bombarded with verbal abuse and react with a smirk. The last ultra-fast-sprint tape-relay of all relays, the last time I will be headquartered in a world I know so much about and believe I am so ready to leave behind.

Not only do I think I'm ready to leave, I think leaving is an act of self-preservation. Maybe I've even convinced myself that it's self- exploration, or self-discovery, or some amazing adventure, either way, a great leap of faith. What I don't know is who I'll discover without the newsroom around me. What I am afraid of-- is figuring out who will emerge when the daily swirl of stress isn't there to distract me.

Who am I, if I am a not a news-gal? A New Yorker? Am I still a New Yorker regardless of where I live? And how will I function without this jolt of daily adrenaline?

Chapter 2: Breathe

The world is a book, and those who do not travel
read only a page ~St. Augustine

Whoever said that travel is the most amazing, mind-expanding experience there is, was so, so right. Actually, it was probably me...

Amazing does begin to explain the amount of over-analytical chatter my brain is currently fighting. My mind's a flurry regarding the promise of travel, my-life, what I'm walking away from... how I got here, and where the hell I'm going.

In a few days, I'll head to France or FRONS as they like to pronounce it. The French are rather particular... meticulous, fussy, even finicky, about their accent and proper pronunciation;

in-fact, it's quite common for them to be totally revolted by an American slant to their mother tongue. If you watch closely, I do believe you can actually see them twitch. Worse yet, they despise those who don't even attempt to speak their language, especially when on their turf.

And then there's me... I'm off, with a vocabulary of approximately seventeen words, bad accent and all, to spend the summer on a small island not too far from Bordeaux... the city of La Rochelle is actually much closer, but either way, it is far from what I know. I've been living in New York City for ten years now, and although I was born and raised in Buffalo, NY, I feel like after ten years, I'm a city-gal. So any island, other than Manhattan, is going to be a real shocker to the system.

This particular island, l'île d'Oléron, is the largest of three small islands in the Atlantic, in the Charente-Maritime Province. It is Frances' second largest island, after well-known Corsica. It also happens to be the island that houses, my new French surfer boyfriend, who I met while traveling in Costa Rica. Trust me- that's a sentence I thought I'd never get to use.

But it's true... undeniably true, I met Philippe when my friend Mary and I traveled to Costa Rica the year before, which happened to be 1992, on a ten day trip. It was an escape oriented vacation to get away from the rat-race of live TV and nightly stresses from cranking out nasty news. So we went to explore a world with monkeys and hiking trails and anything that had nothing to do with our day-in, day-out existence in NY. We hiked the trails, we drank their beer and we met travelers from around the world. Some who were there to escape their lives and live on the edge, and some who seemed to fit in, as if they didn't need to escape any-thing or any place.

Philippe fit-in; he was adorable, extremely handsome and fun, also obviously my polar opposite. He's a French surfer after all... a breed I didn't even know existed, let alone walked the planet. He was extremely relaxed in his manner, as laid back as they come and I, well, I am a typical live TV Production Executive who eats Tums for breakfast. (Lunch, dinner and for my mid-day snack) He speaks five languages… which I find incredibly charming. Aside from French, he manages to get by in Spanish, Portuguese, Italian and English. We got by on a combination of Spanish, English and charades, as well as many smiles and lots of chemistry. What he didn't speak and didn't understand was the concept of rushing or hurrying, that didn't translate to him… in any language.

Perhaps that is why he qualified as the Yin to my Yang. At the time I would have bet millions that I'd never see him again, that it would have been a fun, flirtatious road-fling. But we connected, I was energized by his complete and utter calmness and he fed-off of my high-voltage personality. My time with Philippe seemed magical, maybe because he was a gorgeous French surfer. I'm quite certain that didn't hurt. However, I'd like to think that I was drawn to his essence which invited some kind of inner-calm and joy. I could embrace the quiet when I was with him; I enjoyed finding this calm, easy part of myself there.

The trip made a lasting impression on me, but if truth be told, it was not all because of Philippe. It was the trip itself. It just reminded me there that was life outside of the newsroom. That indeed, there was something else well-beyond Fifth Ave. Huh- who knew?

Not only was calm a big-part of the Costa Rican experience, I learned that some people actually thrived in serene silence. Some people gravitated toward, felt comfortable and even sought out the underdeveloped, slow-paced tranquil surroundings that this small country offered. It was a glorious time; I fed my spirit, rested my body and unwound my over-spun mind. I revived myself while relaxing, recharged myself with lust and it reminded me just how hectic my life was. It reminded me that I didn't want to grow old in a newsroom

Philippe apparently made a connection too, not just to the beauty of Costa Rica, but to the beauty and vivaciousness he found in me. Saying goodbye was difficult.

I returned to my over-charged, highly stressed New York City lifestyle sponsored by a newsroom pumped up on pressure.

Philippe returned to his world too, one that was anchored in calm. He naturally embraced the simple things in life. He had no room for anxiety or stress, he wasn't built that way; perhaps he wasn't even aware that it was a lifestyle that some people, like me, were actually drawn to. We both retreated to our polar-opposite existences and the lives that awaited us.

Much to my surprise, for the following year I would receive poetic letters, care-packages filled with photos of the Island and small gifts and charming notes. He would call me to share delightful stories and it would calm my mind and allow me to escape New York City just by talking to him. In his persistent yet, tranquil manner he began to make himself a part of my life, even from so far away. We began to grow a relationship.

After a year of him writing to me, calling and inviting me to his little French island (Well, technically it's owned by the French Government), I began to see him as a potential boyfriend, an idea I had overlooked originally. He wormed his way into my heart. He began to talk me into coming for a significant visit the Island. And with every heartfelt invitation, I softened to the idea. Philippe had a way, to make a life-changing invitation sound so simple, "Come, be with me, live and see what else the world has to offer." I began to ask myself-why not, instead of why? I had been wanting to have a huge adventure and mix-things-up, and here was my chance. The next time he uttered the words, I actually listened to the offer. He was inviting me to move there, not just to visit. I decided to be open to the concept. It was time to walk away from the madness of Manhattan.

I said "Oui" … if even just for a summer break. So, I decided to go. I decided I could use another infusion of calm and balance. We began to make a plan. And while going to be with him would offer me that certain-tranquility, it would also be an outrageous adventure.

I was sure of a few things, the fact that I would never meet anyone like him hanging around The Upper West Side and that I longed for an escapade as irrational as this. I have often fantasized what it would be like to walk away from my life toward an exotic adventure. In fact, I've come to the realization that I'm on my way to living-out a life-long desire. I have spent endless hours daydreaming about this. I just find it hard to believe that it is actually coming to fruition.

I try not to examine it all too closely because I'm afraid paralysis will set in. If you think leaving New York behind sounds too ridiculous to you, try living it. Right now, I am talking myself down from a massive panic-attack. I'm not sure that the anxiety will lift and there is little comfort in the realization, that I may have actually dreamt this into reality... that might just be part of the scare factor.

I force myself to keep my focus. Besides, this would be my chance to live in France, amongst the French. I'd get a non-touristy view; I imagined I'd be an insider... getting to experience the real-deal. I can hardly believe that as of Friday, I will be in France.

As of now of course, I haven't gotten very far. Truth be told, I am under my covers, fully dressed, with my sneakers on. I've just returned from one last visit with my Upper-West-Side-shrink and then I promptly crawled into my bed, away from the world; I am in a panic. Full blown. Clearly, therapy isn't working.

Today's self-indulgent one-one one session reminds me that I am taking a huge-leap and that this isn't normal. I learned that I am weirder than other Upper West-Siders who all go for therapy, but who don't walk away from their lives in New York City. Apprehension is ripping its way through my veins and I wonder; why did I decide to walk away from my career? How did I decide that leaving my life behind was such a good idea? And how the hell will I get on the plane?

I can't help but wonder... am I insane?

I feel that I know the answer to that last one. At least I knew that I felt crazy, and oddly enough, I was sort-of comforted by that. I felt insane for wanting to leave New York City and even crazier for following through. Well, the follow-through part still remains to be seen. I do have a plane ticket and a few French Francs on the ready, but getting out from under these covers seems to be a huge hurdle. I am, assuming that I will leave my bed... eventually. I guess I am on my way to living-out an extraordinary experience, a journey that is sure to shake things up for me... just as soon as I stop shaking.

First step, I talk myself into lifting my comforter over my head; I peek out to look around my small bedroom and I let my eyes adjust to some light... 'Ah, see... so far so good.' I force myself to step out of my little bedroom and face the fact, that everything is in motion and I am on my way. I look around my Upper West Side Jr. one-bedroom with fondness and fear and I focus on the nonworking, brick fireplace and the exposed brick wall. I feel that every nerve in my body is just as exposed. Breathe. Just breathe.

I try to keep my focus and think about all that is in store for me on l'île d'Oléron.

Chapter 3: Hallucination Vs Reality

A journey of a thousand miles must begin with a single step.
~ Lao Tzu

A traveler without observation is a bird without wings.
~Moslish Eddin Saadi

After traveling for thirty-four hours I must admit to being a tad-bit tired. Actually, I started to get really fuzzy about twenty-hours in. I think I started to hallucinate somewhere (Mid-way) over the Atlantic, but it's hard to tell. I know I didn't sleep a wink on the plane and that by the time I found my way (Proud as I am) to Montparnasse Train Station (Or Gare Montparnasse) it was 7am my time. Well, I guess, it's my time—assuming I am still on New York time. The thing is I don't really know what time I'm on anymore. I'm not certain of much at this point.

Of course, when your flight is delayed by eight hours and you've missed all of your connecting trains, planes and buses and you have been on the road for over thirty-four hours-amazing, or mind-expanding doesn't seem to express the way I am feeling. I just need to go with the flow of it, in all time zones and regroup.

I do know that I'm in Paris... and it is morning, and the smallest garbage trucks I have ever seen are out and about by the time I arrive at the train station. So am I on French time or not? I mean, does that count if I haven't even slept yet? Technically, I think I should still be on NY time. Never mind... I think I might be a little delirious. The point is, (I think) is that I managed to get a ticket on the next train to La Rochelle and to let Philippe know about my change in plans. I keep myself awake on the train ride from Paris down to La Rochelle. I have this fear imbedded in my psyche from a *60-Minutes report,* about gypsy children stealing money; this helps to keep me alert and on-guard. The pure and overwhelming feeling of exhaustion helps to keep my over-analytical drivel at bay; I am just too tired to worry.

I arrive at the small train station and Philippe is here to pick me up; I could see him on the other side of the glass doors. He was leaning against this odd-looking brightly colored, mini-bus, with his hands folded casually across his chest and his face was flush with a big smile. He was wearing a fantastic, beat-up, heavy, black leather coat, a biker-jacket of sorts that looked as if it would help fend off the damp, cool air. He looked severely cute. He looked like he was on cloud-nine. He had this air about him, a sense of calm- that all was right with the world. He seemed completely at ease; he radiated such warmth and exuded a welcoming manner, even from a distance. His face was beaming as I walked toward him; I put my bags down so I could attempt a graceful hello. His thick black hair was spiked upward, which added to his appearance, making him seem more alert and charismatic. Actually- his hair just naturally grew upward, just like a plant grows towards the sun.

I was in a daze, barely awake and anxious at the same time. It occurred to me that he looked so relaxed, he appeared effortless, carefree and it seemed to me, that from his perspective- all of this was completely normal. Despite his calm demeanor, I could tell that he was slightly wound up, excited- or at least relieved that I had finally made it; actually, it was his long embrace combined with the way he kept on looking at me with his beautiful hazel eyes, that gave all of that away.

It seemed to me that he wanted to show me everything, right there, right then. He had waited over a year to share his life with me, his country, his Island, his everything. First, we had to get to the Island which meant we would have to work our way through the narrow city streets of La Rochelle, one of the closest mainland cities to the Island- that had a train station.

He pulled out a map and started to point out all the sights as we began the forty minute ride. I remember we went through what seemed like hundreds of traffic circles and all sorts of curvy, cobblestone streets. There was one old stone building after the next on each tiny, windy road. Even the main roads, ones that were paved, were narrow and crammed with parked cars on either side; the miniature automobiles that are so typical to all of Europe lined the streets. Eventually we approached the breathtaking two-kilometer bridge which would mean we'd be leaving the mainland, the region known as the Marennes. This bridge would bring us to the Island, toward my new adventure.

The bridge suddenly seemed symbolic, it struck me that it connected two different worlds; I was leaving behind the solid ground of the mainland to... to, well that was the question. Where was I going? What was waiting for me there?

The architectural style of the bridge itself is sleek and plain, the structure of the bridge is unique due to its sheer length and the simple, clean-lines was what seemed to define it. The fact that it represented a new-beginning is what made it anything but- simple.

He made a point of showing me the oyster boats below and the fisherman as they pulled up their nets as he pulled out yet another map. It was low-tide and it seemed a bit dusty and quite grey, but intriguing none-the-less. He explained that the difference between high and low tide was rather extreme and very visible on the beaches that surrounded the Island. Or at least I think that's what he is talking about.

He mentions how Fort Boyárd rises in the middle of the sea, half-way between L'île d'Oléron and L'île D' Aix. Once we were on the Island side of the bridge he continued. My mind is in a total fog. I assume he is talking a lot to fill the air, avoid any silent awkward moments. Perhaps he is just really keyed up to finally have me here, he has been waiting a long time and there is a lot to see. The tiny houses that pop up in-between the random vineyards from time to time have a hint of color from the red-barrel tiled roofs, but mostly I notice just how very green everything is. The landscape is otherwise relatively flat, until suddenly a random cathedral appears out of nowhere, piercing the tree-tops with a bell-tower that reaches up to the sky; that is certainly worth pointing out.

I was out of mind exhausted, worn-out and weary and so I just let it roll. His words kept on coming and his tour-guide revelations kept me awake and that was fine, but I was hardly absorbing anything. To me, it gave us something to talk about, something for my mind to focus on, but I knew my recall would be less than zero.

What I didn't realize was that he was actually explaining where I was because that would soon become a very important detail. He would be leaving for work, within an hour. I would be on my own, with the map. He was showing me how I would manage to find my way to where he worked, later.... after I slept. That seemed kind of funny, in that I-haven't-slept-in-two-days kind-of-a-way. When I realized a stick shift mini-van would also be involved, I completely tuned-out. We passed some roosters (I think) and a compact little drive-way area that housed several homes, including the sweetest, tiniest house I've ever seen...

surreal, so surreal that I had arrived. I didn't see it as my home though, it was his house and I was a mere visitor. My mind was in a swirl... did he say stick-shift?

Why pay attention when the details are too...detailed to comprehend? Why listen when the challenges seem too enormous to even consider? I turned off my mind. I was now completely delirious and probably drooling.

I remember that he tucked me in to bed, a bed that was without a box-spring. The mattress was very low to the floor and the pillow top seemed to envelope me, I felt like I had fallen into some clouds and I began drifting away; he told me the map and keys would be on the kitchen table and to meet him at the restaurant where he worked whenever I woke up. At this point, I was so out of it... I agreed. I remember hearing the door shut quietly and that complete darkness took over the T-tiny room.

Being that overtired has an odd effect on me. Somehow my mind and body go into overdrive and it takes me even longer to give up the fight, and let sleep take over. It took me what seemed like forever, to let sleep win and for my mind to release and give in. I had a hard time letting go, all the images of my travels needed to be filed away in the memory section of my mind.

I pictured myself sitting on the floor frustrated at JFK Airport waiting for another update on my delayed flight. I could see myself looking at the French train schedule over and over again and trying to figure out my next best plan. I replayed my entire route all the way through Charles de Gaulle Airport. I remember going through customs and finally making my way through Paris on the airport bus; then I dragged my bags to the train-station itself, so grand. In my mind's eye I could see myself as a passenger on the high-speed train watching the country side fly by with sunflowers and more and more fields of bright, cheerful sunflowers, sunflowers reaching up toward the light, the... and the... and then, I fell into a deep sleep. It was as if I was submerged in water, floating deep into the sea, sunken far below the center of the earth. I felt like I was wading in sludge and my body felt weighted down and yet I felt myself floating and falling at the same time. I was among odd flashes of color and images in a gravity-free place that was my mind- letting go.

Heavy, deep breathing... my lungs filled with air, my body was knocked out and my brain finally had given in, let go. Strange dreams rattled through my mind and I think my psyche needed some much needed rest and repair. When I awoke I had no idea where I was. None.

The room was dark, damp and the stone walls, cemented there long ago did not jog my memory. I knew, or I felt, that this room and these walls had great history and many stories to tell, but my eyes and my mind couldn't really focus yet. The ceiling was exceptionally low and had a wooden beam that cut across the top. I saw a door with a glass window from top to bottom that was covered with a lacey curtain that looked like a big doily; oddly enough head-lights from a car drove right past the other side. I was still somewhere between sleep and conscious thought, I sat up in bed. The covers were heavy although they were made of some fluffy material and the pillow was an odd shape- like a long tube that was the width of the bed.

Where am I?

What planet, what country, what city, what life, what body, what the hell? It almost felt as if I was still dreaming but, as I started to come back to the surface and look around this odd space I remembered where I was. France.

What time is it?

I look around to see if an alarm clock was nearby. I assume that I can now consider myself on French time, although I have hardly adjusted. An old fashioned clock on the night stand says 8:37pm (2:37pm in the afternoon back-home) time to get moving either way.

I take a shower, well I tried- it was the smallest shower stall I'd ever been in, but it did wake me up enough. Enough- at least that I could manage to take the five steps that would lead me to the kitchen; I decided to peak at the dreaded map. There was a note there too with some kind of scribble, I assume they are directions. At second glance, the word 'kitchen' might be an overstatement, it had a counter top across one wall, a half-frig and a little-teeny stove with four burners very close together. I noticed a wood-burning stove close to the wall near the little sink; it looks as if it hasn't been used in decades. A table with four mix-matched wooden chairs separated the kitchen from the living-room. I use the term living-room, lightly.

There was this half bench-like sofa covered in what seemed to be Pleather and it resembled more of car-seat than a couch. Its back was to the kitchen table so it helped to create a new space. Then a low makeshift coffee table and beyond that a stereo tucked into the corner with hundreds of albums stacked in a bookshelf that was built into the wall. The walls in this room looked to have plaster board on them, but I wasn't really sure. That was it. I suppose I'd get the official grand-tour later.

I took a long look at that map, and tried to read his handwriting, even the keys looked different. Oh yea, stick shift... it's all coming back to me. I groaned.

Getting out of the driveway which was surrounded by several of his neighbors' homes was a bit of a riddle unto itself, even though Philippe had obviously parked it so that I wouldn't have to maneuver it too much. Once I was out on the open road, I found mostly curvy and enchanting country streets and I found it a challenge to keep my focus. The fact that I couldn't seem to get the min-van in gear and that I stalled out a dozen times (or so) also tested my focus. I noticed lots of stone houses, farms and a bunch of street signs that had little if absolutely no meaning to me.

It was still light out which added to my sense of uncertainty and jet-lag, I take it all in as I drive (and stall) my way along. The cutest houses I have ever seen dot the landscape. The region's known for three types of homes all that were built prior to World War I. The peasant houses, the fisherman house and the *maison de maître*. I think Philippe's house might be a peasant house because it seems to have the key characteristic which is an outdoor stairway. If I remember correctly. I think that the apartment above is empty now, which makes sense as it isn't high-season yet and I don't remember him saying anything about sharing the driveway. I'll have to ask him later.

Right now I try to picture the map in my mind's eye. Instead I reach over and begin to fumble with it. I stall the mini-van again. People drive-by and wave. I'm not sure if they think they know me or what, but I am embarrassed by my lack of driving skills. I take a good long look at the map and I think I have the rest of the route worked out. I manage to strip whatever was left of the gears and by the end of my journey I stalled that little mini-van about eight more times on what remained of my fifteen minute drive. Do you know they have stop signs attached to actual homes? They just pop up as you are driving along. I took the first parking space I could find which was still about three blocks from the restaurant. I just wanted out-- so parking some place, any place reasonably close to the restaurant was good enough for me.

All of this confirmed what I already knew deep in my very being-- that I was ready for a drink. I couldn't wait for my first, official Island resident drink. I was still so sleep-deprived that it all had a dreamlike quality to it. It's hard to truly wake-up when you are exhausted. It is amazing how fuzzy everything was. I had the sense that I was hallucinating. It was also quite foggy outside and that added to the special-effects-feeling I kept picking-up on.

Everything was old and different... the architecture was unique to the Island and this village square. It was so distinctive, bizarre, and unfamiliar to me. This tiny village of St. Piérre was speckled with the white-washed houses that had either dark or light blue or green wooden shutters mixed-in with ancient stone houses... I am still not sure which way is up.

St. Piérre's allure automatically captivates me. I walked through the town square which is about the size of two city-blocks. It mixes a sense of the present combined with the past, the most modern component I notice are the neon signs. I move my way toward the restaurant, *Le Forum* and I remind myself to let the surreal feeling wash over me. This inviting little village, which happens to be the capital of the Island, is the antitheses of what I am accustomed to. I am reminded that this is the new back-drop to my life. I started to realize that-- I am 'here.' I have actually started my adventure, bizarre indeed. I headed toward the green and white awning of the Italian restaurant as instructed by Philippe and wondered what an Italian restaurant would be like in France.

Little did I know that even the drink choices would leave me some-what confused. My Philippe was working in the kitchen and while he tried to pay attention to me, he was truly too busy to spend too much time at the bar. I call him 'my' Philippe, so as not to confuse him with the nineteen other Philippe-Frenchies he has just introduced me to. I was too much in a fog- to let any of it overwhelm me. Besides, the owner of the restaurant, also a Philippe, is someone I had met back in Costa Rica a year ago, and so we have a reunion ourselves and I am thrilled to see him. It is comforting to see a familiar face and he takes me under his wing. I decide on Champagne. That is a drink I can understand in any language. Hey… wait-a-minute, that's actually a French word… I'll add that to my vocabulary list- - eighteen words and counting.

Regardless, tonight seems like the perfect time, and minimally, as good as time as any, to enjoy some bubbly…

"Champagne, s'il vous plait," I smile at my buddy Philippe. While I am, indeed given a glass of champagne I am also corrected immediately by Philippe, the restaurant owner. Apparently 'vous' is a formal version of you and I need to say tu, (Sounds like too) whenever I am speaking informally. The correction is intended to help me, but my first language lesson pulls me back. I already feel really intimidated to even try my French, and my first phrase out of the gate, is wrong. I make a note to myself to remember to find that little miniature French/English Dictionary I brought with me. I am sure it is somewhere among my things; I think I'll do better if I carry it around with me. No doubt, I'll do a lot of pointing and smiling in the coming days.

My Philippe came out of the kitchen to hand-deliver a heart shaped pizza, as a sort of a welcome. I found that sweet and a tad embarrassing. He was the pizza chef at the restaurant and he made all sorts of odd French style pizzas. I knew he wasn't focused on a big-career and I reminded myself of that. I took in the ambiance- simple and understated, as was my Philippe.

Le Forum boasted a small bar with a metal counter that sat five people. There was an espresso machine in clear view. Wooden tables covered with white-paper were set and small unassuming candles lit the room in an appealing, yet easy manner. Dozens of tables were full of people obviously enjoying their meals. Hundreds of beer glasses each with a different shape and brand names on them lined the shelves above the espresso maker, definitely unique to Europe. The kitchen was beyond that and my Philippe would peek out to look at me from time to time. He had introduced me to everyone and so they tried to come over and speak with me, which was nice, but a challenge with my limited vocabulary, and exhaustion. I felt welcome none-the-less.

I stayed at the restaurant for a little while until my Philippe was free and able to drive us both home, he left his motorcycle behind. I slept for eighteen hours straight. When I finally awoke I felt like I had lost an entire week of my life. My back needed to be stretched out but my mind seemed to be ready to rumble.

I do remember that within mere moments (Ok, I embellished just a bit... let's say within several days) soon after I arrive, and soon after my jet lag began to fade, that I fell in love with the Island, l'ile d'Oléron. This place is extremely charming. I can see why people flock to this little known isle. In fact, it's where many Parisian's 'holiday'. It's kind of a New Yorker's version of Fire Island. Except that there are many key differences between this enchanting French haven and Fire Island.

1. L'ile d'Oléron has way fewer men sporting hairy-backs.

2. Jell-O Shots are hardly a main staple to any French Diet.

3. Fire Island has only a few cars, and in France while they have automobiles- they tend to resemble Tonka trucks. Of course, what the French lack in size, they make up for with serious speed. In fact, Francois Mitterrand actually said that *"Speed is a national sport,"* and that is an understatement.

4. You won't find any summer shares there, with swapped weekends and Long Island Railroad train stubs on the un-swept floor.

5. Circumcised and uncircumcised. Need I say more? Perhaps.

6. The French eat brain, rabbits, and organ meats. Fire Island: Hot Dogs, hamburgers and corn-on-the-cob will do. The French feed that to their pigs by the way—I learned that lesson the hard-way.

7. Marijuana Vs hash

8. Boobs: real Vs fake, exposed Vs not exposed, D-cups, Vs AA-cups.

9. The art of eating, the French have perfected that.

10. On Fire-island it's the art of binge drinking that's the most important and sincerely admired.

11. Smoking is frowned upon in most of The U.S. but sort-of accepted when you are totally drunk. In France, it is a stylish activity in which 85% of the population partakes 100% of the time. It's not part of life, but a way of life.

12. Kissing hello: once, twice, three times, four times?

These and other observations are firing off in my brain, it's as if I have to review, inhale, absorb and take in all the difference of my new world in-order to adapt. And I also notice that I have no one with whom to share my running commentary with, my growing catalogue of reflections. This was actually kind of a lonely thought for me to acknowledge.

Sure, I could tell Philippe about them but he won't understand. I know, I know, how cliché to have a Frenchman in my life named Philippe. You have to be an American though to understand just how cliché, and how ridiculous that and everything seems. You need to be a fish-out-of-water with other out watered fish nearby with whom to share your feelings.

Well, I am the token American on the Island and there isn't another American in sight for hundreds of miles. Remember, it's 1993 and the Internet is basically nonexistent. There is no such-thing as Skype, instant messaging, emailing or staying connected on the cheap. A ten-minute phone call to The States requires a land-line or phone-booth and is about $40 dollars (U.S.) Add to that I am six-hours ahead (time-wise) so sharing jokes is not only expensive, I find it wildly inconvenient too!

My entire life I've enjoyed making observations and people always have seemed to value that, I'm always being told how funny I am. (Despite the fact that you may or may not agree at this point.) Bottom line is, that I have this ongoing inner-dialogue, these thought-flashes, that I like to bring to an outer dialogue to help confirm this new reality I am living. Minimally, it seems to somehow validate the experience for me.

Here I am, on this Island that is ripe with material, and I have no one with whom to share. It seems to me to be a cosmic joke of sorts, having all of these new thoughts, insights and experiences to share and no-one to share them with. I have this sensation of having some real comedy and amazing stories piling up in my brain and not one person, to chat with who will truly understand.

I'm juggling jokes that are over-loading my mind without one English speaking person to address. How can I express all these bottled up ideas, and why do I find that necessary? I don't know- but it seems like that is one of the best parts of any journey, sharing.

You see, you really have to be a stranger in a strange land, to get it, to understand how 'off' everything appears to be. Perhaps being a nice Jewish gal from Buffalo makes me strange, but way beyond that, it certainly makes me a stranger to the life of the well- traveled European vacationer. Growing up in my family, vacations meant a visit to my cousins in Brooklyn or in Hartford, CT. The word 'exotic' usually didn't come into play there.

Oh… and I've been to Niagara Falls many more times than the average person. I suppose that makes me unique, but worldly? Hardly…technically, not even close. Aside from the ten years of New York City under my belt, I've seen a bit here and there. If anything, my now-and-again voyages were just enough to make me want more and to show me just how sheltered and inexperienced I really am.

The times I've traveled have always inspired me. I've never been able to sleep. The fresh experiences and brief glimpses at a new world tend to feed my brain that acts like it's hopped up on Starbucks espresso. For a non-caffeine consuming gal, this means restless nights to be sure.

Right at this very moment, my mind reels. Too many good stories and funny comments cram my overloaded brain. So many new experiences, great visuals, interesting happenings and fresh faces cross my path. Everything is novel, what others may consider as the mundane details please and uplift my spirit. My psyche takes it in and feeds on the newness and freshness of every distinct moment… and makes me think. It's what travel is all about for me, being out of my day to day routine and living in an alternate universe. All of that swirls in my mind and needs an outlet…and that, my dear reader, is what brings me to you.

You see, I have to get this stuff out of my head or I'll never sleep again. It's like a stand-up comedy act that won't sit down until I share it with someone. Guess what, reader? You have the *bon chance* to be my imaginary travel companion. Dear reader, you are my very new friend, the person who I can turn to and say, 'Did you see that'?

Just so you can understand how much I need to get this off my chest; the very same chest that will be exposed to the French sun later this week, which is giving me countless anxiety attacks and a dreadful sense of apprehension that we'll get to later and just so you understand how desperate I am to share this with someone, (That would be you, dear reader, you) it is 1:30am in the morning, in France (that makes it 7:30pm ET) and I am cracking myself up in bed replaying my extraordinary, bizarre-o day in this poles-apart universe, called my new life. My Philippe is sleeping and I am going to have to crawl out of bed or wake him up and force some bad-ass story on him that he won't find funny or endearing at all.

Nope, it's clear… the choice is made. Out of bed I go in search of a quiet well-lit place… and into the WC (Water closet) it is. It is actually the only room in the house with a door that I can shut behind me so I won't disturb him. So here I sit on a toilet, the likes of which I've never seen before, so I can write my heart out and empty my over-loaded head.

I hope you appreciate the sleepless nights and the toilet-office imagery, because I sure do. And I'm praying that you find my life here as amusing as I do.

Chapter 4: In the Fast Lane

The world is round and the place which may seem like the end may also be the beginning. ~ *Ivy Baker Priest*

Just to set the record straight, before I got to this island I lived on the island of Manhattan on The Upper West Side, 85th Street between- West End and Riverside Drive, to be exact. I took taxis, walked and forced myself to ride the over-crowded subways. I can remember tightly closing my eyes shut just so I wouldn't have to look at the person that was less than an inch from my face. Oh, the horror of it, how I detested that morning commute. I hated having strangers pressed up against my body. (At least buy me dinner First.)

I had ample opportunity to just sit and think about stuff like that the first few days on the Island. In fact, I found that my newfound solitude was quite distracting and sometimes even slightly disturbing. I realized just how fast life had been for me. I felt like I had so much space on the Island and for some reason-maybe due to the space or the quiet, or the obvious contrast, this was the first time that I could sit and reflect on the life I had been leading for almost a decade.

I worked my tail off at NBC. I worked in news: live, crazy, bleed-when-it-leads, NEWS. The last four years I had been part of the start-up team for CNBC. Launching a cable network is pretty intense, kind of like giving birth to quintuplets day after day, or so I would guess. This meant when a plane crashed or the market crashed my life went from full speed ahead to out-of-control hyper mode. And the only way to unwind was to party hardy. I ran all over that city, day and night. Parties here, clubs there, friends and more friends everywhere. Add to that I was a dating machine. At the time it seemed like I would meet guys everywhere. Out and about on the streets of Manhattan, at book-stores, out on shoots... you name it. Men, men, dates, dates, friends and more friends meant I was a social animal in a city that kept the pace. The city that never sleeps was enough to keep me, an avid lifelong insomniac, busy and easily entertained.

When I first arrived in New York City, I was reasonably sheltered. I had lived a quiet, average suburban (tree-driveway-tree-driveway) kind of a teenage life, and then I headed to college, where I went for the party and ended up with a diploma. New York was bigger than life, and in the past ten years, I had actually grown up enough, expanded my world enough, to fit in. I was a big-city gal, I knew my way around. I shopped at Zabars (The best, super-high-end-yuppy yummy grocery store on the planet) and Central Park was my very own backyard. New Yorkers usually believe they know it all and have seen it all. But I knew there was something else out there I wanted to touch, to taste, to see...I wanted it all. I wanted something that would shake up my world and jiggle my brain out of its daily rituals. I was just too busy at the time to figure out what that might be.

My life was chaotic, sponsored by... live news, tons of friends, going out every night, theater, cinema, concerts, festivals, happy hours, farmer's markets, museums, galleries, Central Park and Sunday brunches. I was truly a social-queen, I lived and breathed New York City and worked hard, as all good New Yorkers do. Yet I was ready for a change, and a major-one at that.

My life was the-fast-lane, incredibly fast. Man, it was New York City after all! But this fast crazed, over run, over-the-top never rest life is what I had come to know... my norm was fast, faster and fastest. To me, going 'Upstate', laughingly defined by the average New Yorker as anything north of 175th Street, was necessary for mental stability. But to me, it would be an overnight trip at most. Off to the countryside I'd go- screaming my way out of New York City in some rent-a-wreck car, to grab some fresh air for about seventeen hours to hurry back for whatever calendared event was scheduled next. That intense exercise in driving over the George Washington Bridge, to Woodstock, or New Paltz, was my version of 'relaxation.'

So now, being on this teeny tiny Island that was so still and so silent, this was going to turn me around totally and that seemed extreme. It was the pure slowness of it all that amazed me and shocked my city-girl system to the core. The sluggishness of my new life forced a new perspective-- now that was radical! For the first time in my life, at thirty, I'm slowing down. I'm not even sure I know how to do that but I'm going to give it a fair shot. I guess I have little choice out here on this tiny-Atlantic island. I am going to be happily unemployed. Me the workaholic, will not be working.

And most importantly I'll be very far away from everything and everyone I know and love. And I do mean... everything I know. Toto we are not in Kansas anymore. Note; no-one here knows who Toto is either.

To make things seem even more dramatic, my new life will take place in a new language, one I do not speak...yet. So it really seems like I am taking some giant leap into some vortex, some alternate world. The language and scenery change really help to add to the sense of the surreal and to the severity of the contrast. I am now on the other side of the Atlantic, perhaps in another dimension, in a culture that embraces *slow* just as much as New Yorkers embrace FAST.

I've already gone to the beach here and found myself looking over the vast expanse of the water. As I gaze over the Atlantic Ocean I wonder how it is possible that my polar-opposite life, the very one I used to live just days ago... still exists on the other side.

My new life has me stationary, static, still and basically motionless. It also has me parking a mini-van right in our garden. Cars and gardens are not something NY-ers have. Not Manhattanites, there just isn't enough space for it. This particular automobile, just so you know, is a 1979 Renault Van.... bright, bright green, a toxic looking thing with a stick shift that has a mind of its own, on its last-legs. The van and the stick shift is entirely another thing I am trying to get used to. Oh, and to get in and out of the little tucked away teeny tiny baby house, I'll drive past my neighbor's roosters, which apparently was not a hallucination, as I had first suspected. Roosters... and I think a few pigs too.

I think I need some time to adjust, so I'll use the quiet and the stillness to hone in and find my center, my modest pace... I'll do my best. It is damned quiet here; most of the visitors will come later in the summer months so now it is primarily locals and weekenders with homes here. The pristine beaches, protected dunes and exceptional wildlife, including tons of rare birds, are about all there is here. Oh yes, the oyster beds and those that work in the oyster industry make up a lot of the year-round residential base of this Island on the southern side of the Pertuis d'Antioche Strait. Lots of windsurfers, fisherman, farmers and surfer-types abound, but they are all basically quiet too. That doesn't mean there aren't nightclubs and restaurants to keep you entertained, there are... but it is just as easy to be quiet and calm. Those who don't farm or fish for a living but live here fulltime, own hotels, shops and restaurants that cater to the tourists and they make up the balance of the population here.

Living among surfers and oyster-fishermen is clearly way-out of my norm. And while I am just getting started I am continuously reminded that this is an exploration of everything I do not know. This is an extreme difference, a contrast of everything that I call home. Everything that I do, all that I think I am, has now been turned on its side. I am uncertain of what will be revealed. That is exactly what I say I've been wanting. And now, God help me... here it is!

Friday in France

Chapter 5: The French Kiss

A kiss is the shortest distance between two.
~ Henny Youngman

Boy those French, they have a different word for everything.
~Steve Martin

Kissing is something I'd like to think 'I know.' Doesn't everybody? I mean really, everyone thinks they're a good kisser, but we know the truth to that. We have all had the misfortune of kissing a bad kisser at least once in our lives. Therefore, some- one, somewhere is overestimating their kissing ability. Perhaps, I digress.

Let's get back to the basics on this. I believe everyone knows the difference between a basic-greeting kiss and a passionate kiss, i.e. your new lover-kiss. I also know that what we call *French Kissing* has nothing to do with how the French kiss. Stay with me here. Of course, when you are intimate with someone, you are intimate with them and your kisses reflect that. Call that the French Kiss if you like, as long as you do it well, that's all anyone should really care about. The French don't call that a French Kiss by the way and for some reason I think that's important to note.

Kissing is one of my first cultural lessons in France. Not a bad place to get a start with my worldly education, indeed! To clarify I'm talking about the hello kiss and the ever-popular goodbye kiss, that take place in France. (Neither considered the French-Kiss). I'm talking about the, holy-crap, how many times do I have to kiss you, kiss?

The first tutorial I come across is this; I learn that you only kiss people hello the *first* time you see them that day. Why? I don't know, but you should not kiss someone hello, more than one-time, per-day. But you *always* kiss them goodbye regardless of how many times you have seen them. A tad detailed perhaps, but really easy to follow the rule once you've been introduced to it. Either way - good to know.

You also kiss people hello, (At least on Oléron) that you *don't* know. Meaning strangers, however only if they are in the company of others that you *do* know (and kiss). So to review... not random strangers, but rather strangers that are randomly with someone you would other-wise greet with a kiss.

Add to that, in France they have different kissing rules based on what part of the country you are from; specifically the number of kisses offered at any hello or goodbye moment. The number of times you kiss someone is determined by the region they come from. Parisians kiss four times; that's to your right, *kiss*, to the left, *kiss*, to the right, *kiss* and to the left, *kiss*. People from the Island only kiss twice; that's a mild lean to your right, *kiss*, to your left *kiss*, and bam, you're done. Folks from the mainland of France (Other than Paris) kiss three times (Right, *kiss*, left-*kiss*, right, *kiss*) dismount---done. Often times there is a slight hesitation there for beginners... unclear on how many kisses are appropriate. The thing is this is even confusing for The French. Me, I'm completely clueless.

Is it inappropriate to use my right hand to keep a tally? Most likely. Four, three or two- depending on location seems a lot more challenging for my tiny-brain to embrace, a lot more than a casual hug or hand-shake, but when in Rome...

No matter how many kisses you offer you usually say 'Ca va?' At the same time... which is a catch-all greeting meaning basically *how's it going?* Fine, I am confident that I've got it.

If you do not know the person you're kissing, (A stranger who is with others you do know) then you say, 'Enchante' (Roughly meaning, nice to meet you...literally it means, enchanted). Mid-kiss you also mumble your name as you move from cheek to cheek. No real time in that case to say *Ca va*. So you establish that it is indeed nice to meet them and then you tell them who you are... all during the actual kiss-exchange. Excellent, great, good... got it.

In New York City we typically kiss and hug our friends. A hug-hello or offer to shake hands to those we don't know. A casual wave will do for everyone in-between, or for those that fit neither group, or for those whose hands look really too unappealing to touch, as well. So, generally in New York City it goes like this: a *kiss*, (Right or left is not typically specified) you just go for the 'big lean in' then warm-embracing- hug, and then- pat-pat, usually twice- on the back. Done. For large crowds, a big general wave will cover everyone, nice.

A lot of ground work can be bypassed with the almighty wave, it covers a lot of people in a short period of time. It's socially acceptable and easy, simple. Oh, I like the big wave for a large group. That's a friendly greeting and what I've come to learn very recently, is a huge time saver as well. I hadn't realized I had a love for the wave until now. I believe that if for some reason waves were banned and removed from our social rule-book, everyone else would realize how much they'd miss the wave too. A powerful time-saver underestimated by those of us who take it for granted. Oh how I miss the hug and wave conceptually and in-practice.

No hug by the way. No hug, ever, not for goodbye or hello when it comes to the French that is. Perhaps there are one or two exceptions... if you are really, really, really close, or exceptionally sad, or are going away for an extremely long period of time and you feel compelled, and the moon is in the summer solstice than you can hug. But as a normal, traditional, act-as-if you know what is going on, follow the laws of the land- everyday kind of a greeting, never hug.

As an American, I didn't realize how heavily I relied on the casual-yet warm-hug. Hugging was part of my genetic makeup... I guess I'll have to put that aside for now, my hug-imbedded... Pavlov-type response. Ah the hug, apparently, a habit that I'm finding just a bit difficult to let go-of. Awkward too, I might add- to say the least, when you stop while you are in a mid-hug-approach. Suddenly aware that your arms are located up in the air and you have to re-set.

Let's review the rules I've learned thus far to see if I am really ready to tackle greeting people. OK so, not only do I need to know if I've seen them yet today or not; which on a small island, you see the same people over and over again, so to keep track- may sound easy – but trust me- it ain't. Perhaps even more important is that I need to keep track and record in my memory their geographical-kiss orientation, which will then indicate to me the proper number of kisses which would be either two, three or four.

Hell, sometimes while folks are mid-kiss people actually ask, how many? People will say 'trois, quatre?' (Three-four?) Hopefully they'll answer mid-the second-kiss, so you'll know if you are to proceed to the next side for the remaining third kiss or perhaps even a forth. If the answer isn't timely, it's awkward anyway and you're at a total loss. And of course, no hugs... well that one is hard to get accustomed to, but easy to remember, now isn't it?

Eventually you'll actually start to remember where people are from, which clears up who kisses how many times, and hopefully you'll start to note who you've already kissed that day. But this is work and effort my friend! And let me remind everyone, I'm on vacation here!

OK, now… imagine this. You enter a restaurant. You know approximately twenty-three people there; twenty-one of them you haven't seen since yesterday, you think, but you can't be sure… and they are with two extra people you've never met. Let the kiss fest-test, begin.

My Philippe used to work in a restaurant, so running into twenty or thirty people I knew, was a common occurrence, even the first week. I knew the entire wait-staff, the chef, the owner and about ten to twenty-five of the patrons. Or at least I'd been introduced to them at least once, which put them on my kiss-list, regardless. This is a small and very friendly island. Even at the very beginning of my time on l'ile d'Oléron, I felt the need for Chap Stick.

So on a typical night; I'd walk in and start with the… to your right, *kiss*, to your left *kiss*, and a quick glance into my mind's-kiss-folder, and yes… I know this person is from the Island, so good, I'm done. NEXT: kiss to your right, to your left, to your right (Ask mid-way trois ou quatre?) four is the response, so four it is; and to your left for the final kiss. I almost feel like a special dismount would be appropriate as if some Russian judge is grading me off on the sidelines, but I suppose not. So I move down the bar: to your right, *kiss*, to your left *kiss*, (Another Islander, moving on) NEXT: kiss to your right, to your left, to your right then ask mid-way trois ou quatre? Three it is, and we're done; well technically I am done with only four people.

Maybe this would be a good time to institute a lip-stretch, you know some kind of warm up exercise so I don't cramp up or something hideous like that. A little lip time-out for beginners… but hell, my goal is to blend in with the locals and so I forge ahead.

Do you understand, the time, the energy we are talking about here? Let me remind you of the anti-wave policy in place; no big wave for large groups, no waves ever, not even with a 'Hi' or friendly 'nod' attached to it. It's a huge kissing extravaganza. I've got another…well let's see, this takes a minute to calculate: twenty-one out of the twenty-three I haven't seen yet today. But I don't want to insult the other two I may have seen earlier (I don't remember) so OK, figure twenty-three minus the four I've covered already, plus the two extra people I don't know… so OK that's nineteen plus two. So even if I am only going on an average kiss estimate and that means I need to kiss each person three times; (Time out, I need a calculator) I've got fifty-seven kisses, no wait… sixty-three kisses remaining. No joke.

I think The French should have the kiss named after them, even if it isn't that kind of kiss. Holy shit, they've earned it. They've turned hello and goodbye kissing into some kind of Olympic sport. Or at least it should be. And if it were, I imagine it to be part of the track and field competition… a relay or a marathon, perhaps a combo. Because let me tell you, stamina is involved. Regardless, they'd sweep the gold metal year after year.

So now I've greeted everyone I need to. I try not to really look around to confirm that fact, because if I drudge up a few extra people I'll have to continue this; right now I feel truly, ridiculous –really, enough. Besides, I'm hungry. I came to the restaurant to eat, to drink and to see people move about and to avoid staring at the walls in the house… not to kiss twenty-three people; but you have-to get past the greeting before you can do anything else.

So I settle in for my apéritif and visit with friends. Keep in mind; anytime someone else walks in or out of the restaurant, whom you haven't seen yet that day, or who is leaving for the night, you have to kiss. So it is kissing in perpetual motion, it can and will begin again and again and actually it never ends. Indeed, it never really stops long enough to have to start again. So even if you are officially settled-in with all of your hello kisses behind you, you will still encounter many more kisses, and so it goes. Let's assume on average, every ten minutes that at least four people that you know enter or leave the restaurant, on a slow night. So that's another twelve kisses per ten minutes minimum; which adds up to six times per hour, that's seventy-two kisses an hour on your down-time.

Ten O'clock already and my Philippe is finally done with work. I've only been at the restaurant an hour and half. I look around the room. At least seven people I know have left. However four new people arrived. So let's see- that was twenty-three plus the two previously unknowns, minus seven, equals eighteen plus the four additional people who arrived after me, putting it back up to twenty-two. Remember that means twenty-two sets of goodbye kisses, on average of three kisses per person. You always kiss goodbye, regardless.

I have sixty-six kisses, between me and the door and so does Philippe. Let's face it, as a couple we have 132 cheek-kisses, between us and our exit. And where are we headed? Just down the street to a nightclub where we will see almost every one of these people within an hour! Luckily we will not have to greet them again at the club... oh but we will, indeed- kiss them goodbye again. Details, details.

Do you see why I am awake at night? Do you see? Just the math alone, I have to calculate all this before I can let my insomniac oriented brain lay to rest. I don't know about you reader, but my lips are tired! And secretly I am missing the hug. The 'ole pat-pat on the back, combined with a small embrace that I left back in Nuevo York. I guess I should get out of bed just to apply Chap Stick.

Don't get me wrong, I make fun of it, only because I love it. I am amazed only because it is so different from what I know, and different is what I came to experience. Even the insanity of it, the time-consuming-ness of it, makes me laugh. How can you not adore the way the French kiss hello? It's so... uhm, so... French.

Friday in France

Chapter 6: Change Please

All changes, even the most longed for, have their melancholy; for what we leave behind us is a part of ourselves; we must die to one life before we can enter another. ~Anatole France

When you are through changing, you are through.
~Bruce Barton

I knew when I left New York that I had very few goals in mind. The point after all, was to leave any pressure and stress behind, which included goals. I did however, have a few minor things that I wanted to accomplish. First I want to learn the language, so I would have to put my embarrassment behind me. Second, I want to really learn what life is like on the Island and third, I want to get healthy. I want to lose weight and feel great in every way, shape or form. Since it became clear to me right away that my Philippe would be working a lot this gave me plenty of time to do all this. Even though I didn't want a schedule, I knew I needed to create some kind of plan and some way to create a life for myself. I assume I'll get busier with friends as I get more comfortable... eventually, or so I hope. Early on, I fell into a semi-routine of nothingness.

Philippe would wake up when he was about to leave the house and kiss me goodbye and I'd usually roll back over and drift into sleep. Once I did get up though I would do a minimum of ninety-minutes of exercise. Mostly sit-ups and weight lifting, by weight-lifting I mean, I would use two large water bottles and do some odd-looking calisthenics. Then I would take the bike out for a thirty-sixty minute spin and check out the Island. Each day I would venture further and further away from the tiny house and hope I'd find my way back. I would also walk to the beach and take in the fresh air. Despite all of this activity, I still have a lot of time on my hands. Luckily Philippe would come home in the late afternoon and we'd have a wonderful reunion. The kind of reunion a new relationship appreciated and probably what the French siesta schedule is made-for. We would crawl into our bed and savor every minute together. Then he'd go back to work which would leave me with more time on my hands.

I did enjoy the amazing garden. I would park myself on the stairs that led to the empty apartment above us, or sit on one of the mismatched chairs at the rickety table to read. I was quickly running out of reading material though, so I decided to be adventurous and hit one of the book stores. I figured St. Piérre would be the best place to go because it was the only area I sort of knew my way around. The village bookstore had ten, maybe twelve books in English, three from Mary Higgins Clark, two from Tom Clancy and a few cheesier looking romance novels as well. I had read most of them or I was not intrigued by the balance.

I was excited to see a collection of newspapers but quickly discovered that they were in French, German, Spanish or Italian. It's really hard to begin to grasp news in another language, nearly impossible, especially when you have no idea how to read and the photographs really only tell a small part of the story. I was going through a news-junky withdrawal. Not only did I used-to produce the crap, I was an avid reader and consumer of news. I did try to glean news from every source that I could. I got my information from people at the restaurant. I'd either ask the Chef or ease-drop on strangers around me. All dangerous ways of consuming news-understanding only bits and pieces... it really left me in a fog. That became difficult to deal with and it frustrated me even more, for a variety of reasons; mostly, because I couldn't understand what I was being told, even with my little dictionary to assist and also because it was such a far-cry from my newsroom days; I did miss Associated Press and Reuters Wire-Service access, that was for sure.

Through a rousing game of charades with the nice bookstore owner and with the aid of my trusty one-inch tiny French/English Dictionary, I did learn that an English newspaper and maybe even a few new English books could be had within a few weeks or so, during high-season, once some British tourists arrived. Joy! Also she directed me to an English book on the history of the Island, made for tourists, it was the only other book in English they had. So I picked that up and I also decided to buy a copy of Les Trois Petits Cochon (*The Three Little Pigs*) and I returned to the garden to get some reading done.

I cannot tell you how annoyed I was trying to get through *The Three Little Pigs*. It was a struggle and rather humbling to come to the realization that *The Three Little Pigs* is a book far beyond my language skills. I tossed it aside; I had to put it down for another time once my skills improved a bit. My ego was bruised, rather badly.

Forced to read the one book I now had at my disposal- I learned that the Island had an interesting history, although typically I am not that interested in history. I guess it helped me feel like I was doing something valuable with my time, it was that or Tom Clancy.

Apparently, l'ile d'Oléron, was actually connected to the main continent at one time (Pretty cool) and they have some kind of proof of that. Also the book explained that people existed here during the ice age. That was impressive. Then the evidence jumps a bit (Or I skip a chapter or two) to The Middle Ages, which is fine by me. This is when the Island was in the hands of Geoffroy Martel and then the Ducs-d'Aquitaine.

At the end of that Middle Ages and until the 15th Century the Island went back and forth between the Brits and the French. The last part of the 15th Century there was quite a bit of violence. Some type of revolt by the folks who produced salt who were (apparently) very opposed to and upset by tax increases. This made me think that the more things change, the more things stay the same. This also made me think that I should give *The Three Little Pigs* another try. Salt-tax wars are not my thing.

Then of course, there were a lot of religious wars in Europe and the Island was strategically located enough so that the Catholics and the Protestants would fight over it. And while the French Revolution did not affect Oléron greatly, it was a turning point to the more modern history. Roads were made that linked the Château-D' Oléron to Saint-Denis-D' Oléron, two of the now larger villages on either end of the Island. I learned that from 1940 until 1945 Oléron was occupied by German forces, and that it was liberated by the French troops when they landed in the middle of the night on April 30, 1945. And I learned that in French history after 1945, that they really don't consider it history anymore, but rather part of their modern-day story.

Reading about these aspects of Oléron was enough to inspire me to hit the road and do a little exploration myself. After all, how long would I let that mini-van intimidate me and ruin my grand ambitions?

Enough, I decide I am ready to make my own history. So I plan in the coming days to explore a different town or village. The weather was reasonably crappy and it gave me something to do, a goal and a purpose. I had to cover approximately 175 square kilometers (Whatever that is).

I knew that the Island had fifteen communities but really eight main villages spread throughout.

- La Brée-les-Bains

- Le Château

- Dolus-D' Oléron (This is the town that we live in although we are in the village of Le Deux; our village is probably no more than seventeen-twenty houses, so I don't know how that qualifies as a separate place but- who am I to argue?)

- Le Grand-Village-Plage

- Saint-Denis

- Saint-Georges

- Saint-Piérre (Where Le Forum is and the capital of the Island.)

- Saint-Trojan

So once I learned that Le Deux, the tiny village of fifty, where I was living was actually part of the larger area known as Dolus, a place I used to pass a sign for, on my way to St. Piérre, I decided that it was a good place to start. I also voted against the mini-van and I rode my bike there instead.

Each main village has a Rue Piétons; a street for walking, where no-cars are allowed. This is where the main commerce is and usually if large enough, has the town square etc. There wasn't that much to Dolus but as with all small French villages, it had an allure and an appeal that I am undeniably drawn to and charmed by, none-the-less. The windy Rue Piéton had cute shops and a beautiful church that dated back quite some time. I round it off like that because 15th or 16th Century architecture is not my specialty and I find it all romantic, intriguing and peaceful regardless. That and the fact that I left my history book at home encouraged me to just admire it and categorize it as old. The thing is, I'm more of an-explore-for-yourself kind of a gal Vs a read and memorize about it kind-of-a lady.

Of course there was the Boulangerie to buy fresh bread and places to buy coffee, but once I had explored and walked the entire village, I found myself heading back home. The entire center village was really only a few city blocks long, so my exploration time was quite short. After this initial trip to Dolus, I would stop by from time to time to mix things up a bit, but I usually ended up in St. Piérre. There, I knew people and that made it a more interesting place to hang out. From that day forward though, I went to a different village each day, some I found more interesting than others. Each day I would make an effort to learn something new, try to advance my French and keep myself entertained.

Often though, I would spend my nights at the restaurant hanging out because it felt comfortable there and of course, I could get a few moments with my Philippe as well. If not at Le Forum, I found people extremely excited to invite me to their homes for dinner too. Awkward as that was for me, especially at the beginning, it was really quite nice, and so I would go. I did all that I could to keep myself open to discovering and not to fall into a rut. I was after all on the other side of the Atlantic, who knows when I'll be back again.

Chapter 7: Foreign Men

I like Frenchmen very much, because even when they insult you they do it so nicely. ~*Josephine Baker*

I have a thing for foreign men, always have. Perhaps it is their accent, their charismatic way and the fact that they have lived such a different life. All I know is historically speaking, if I am within earshot of an accent I automatically turn to look. My friends watch for it, it is like a Pavlov's response, stronger than my hug-addiction, if truth be told. My head spins automatically in the direction of the voice-with-an-accent, in hopes that a cute face is part of the package.

Back home, my friends like when I date foreigners because then, when I am telling stories I imitate them with their accent and all. It kind of gives more flavor, texture, a little spice to my stories. I tend to perform my stories for the ladies, so an accent helps to add a little depth of character to my schpiel. What the hell, a good story teller can always use a little shtick. All that aside, I am attracted to the foreign man as a concept.

Perhaps it is the cultural difference I embrace, or their style, their confidence, their interest in American women, I don't know exactly. It is something I was born with. Before I met Philippe I had dated guys from: Spain, Belgium, Holland (At least two) several Brits, Israelis, a few Greeks, a few Germans and hmmm, I am sure I am forgetting a few, but you get the idea. They all had a unique charm and charisma that I rarely found in the all-American boy-next-door, although I dated plenty of them too I suppose. Maybe I like men who can't argue well in my language. Whatever it is, it has been on a serious trend for many years now… I'll call it a flare for the exotic. I like to consider myself a U.N. dater or the Statue of Liberty of love… there I am in the harbor, *Bring me your tired, your poor, your international hotties….*

I'm not sure whether it is bad or good-but what I do know is that through all the differences they have a lot in common too. Their 'maleness' shines through, those common characteristics that are Y-chromosome based. Y chromie-specials… at least to the men I've dated. For example the apparent need to be in command of driving. You know, when your guy is behind the wheel of any car, he is the captain of that ship… he is at the helm. He will fake his way through directions, car troubles and even be in charge of tuning in the radio stations. He will not admit to defeat. In fact, I always wondered how they knew their way around so well. How was it possible that they never were lost? It's not. They are lost, everyone knows it- they just won't ask for directions.

I always thought no matter who you were dating a great test of the potential success of the couple would be to give the duo really bad directions and see how well they do. Just offer up bad directions (No GPS allowed) and see if true love takes its course. Bottom line is if the couple lives to tell about it then they can marry; if not whoever comes out alive can publish a book, or sell the movie rights telling the tale of their last and final hours together. My guess is, the second you hand over the bad directions; depending on how bad they actually are, you might as well start separating your stuff, and get it over with.

I was used to spending time with foreign men in New York City, and I was the local, I felt like I knew my way around and could tell when we were in trouble or lost. But in France, Philippe could BS me all the way in a big circle and I would have no idea. Especially at first, I couldn't read the signs and one old stone or brick building on a cobble stone street started to look the same as the next after a while. So we never got to have the official *We Are Lost* fight, that in some way it is a right- of passage, a milestone for any couple. What we did get to have was a fight over gear shifting. Another car-oriented, male, Y-chromie item, the, I can drive better than you thing. Ridiculous.

Mind you, I never claimed to be able to really shift gears well, but I just don't see the point in yelling about it either. I mean, now I'll be all nervous and I will probably forget about the clutch altogether, and that can't be good for either one of us. To be fair in this case, I somehow managed to shift right past third gear... oh, and I probably should mention I forgot to take the emergency break off too. That's kinda bad 'eh? He starts mumbling French swear words, but I recognize enough of them to know this is not going to be a fun outing.

Why isn't he driving? Maybe he is testing me. Ah well, too late for that. Now all I keep thinking is RELAX and I telepathically send him my very-best 'relax-vibe messages,' as if that is actually going to calm him down. For a very calm, cool man, he is started to get ruffled and that feels worse than if you are with someone who is naturally a hot-head. But it takes my focus further away from my driving and I hear squeaks as I get into the fifth and last gear. Thank goodness, I think and I breathe a sigh of relief. Let's just pretend none-of that happened and we'll continue our outing. He tries to continue to give me pointers half in French, half in English and I think he tried a little bit of Spanish too. And I tried to gain my focus.

Would an American guy be so uptight about bad gear-shifting? Probably, oh-well... we have to take the good with the bad. All I know is, from now on, when we are together, he drives.

Chapter 8: The Gift

Gravitation is not responsible for people falling in love.
~Albert Einstein

Yes, Philippe would have to drive from now on, I decided and I thought that was an excellent decision. Sadly it lasted only until the following day. The Chef that Philippe worked with, Daniel apparently had a gift for us; it was a car he wasn't using. Who gives a car as a gift? Really? Apparently, the Chef and his wife do, and I found it amazing and quite touching.

We simply had to pay for the papers, arrange to get them in order, and it was ours, well really it was for me to ramble around the Island with. It was a Renault hatchback and a very generous gift at that. I was hoping I wouldn't have to put it in gear in front of anyone. Philippe had a better idea; I would drive it away and he could torture me with a gear-shifting lesson, sponsored by our recent driving situations, this time with an audience.

Suddenly he is the parent. A French parent and I am the slow and sincerely gear-shift-handicapped child. Now, I am trying to be joyous about this gracious gift, but having Philippe harp all the way home is taking some pleasure out of the moment. I decide to create our first international-couple rule. Anyone can borrow it if they need to.

Rule #1-

We will not discuss driving, gears, clutches, breaks or anything remotely related to automobiles, other than, 'isn't that a cute color'.

The rule was accepted (Kind of the Geneva Accord for us) and we drove home quietly... both searching our memory bank for the 'ah love' category, I'm sure. How such a stupid moment can take away all the grandeur of love is beyond me. But as a witness to this, and the one who is actually shifting in my car-seat pissed off, I will attest to it.

We get home and talk about how nice it was of the Chef to give us the car. Philippe and I decide that on his next day off that we'll go to the Bureau D' Automobiles. This makes the DMV look like a picnic. Anyway- we'll go and straighten out the paper work, which if I understand correctly includes a green card, a pink card and a gray card. One is for insurance... the other is for... I don't know. I'll tag along and one thing is for sure... HE can drive.

Chapter 9: Beach, Boobs & Kisses

No matter where you go… there you are. ~Anonymous

If you want to succeed you should strike out on new paths, rather than travel the worn paths of accepted success. ~John D. Rockefeller

Just the idea of going to the beach with all Philippe's friends and having my boobs there with me… well, not just with me but, the technicality of having them out in the open before me and exposed to the world… gave me more anxiety than you might imagine. That's how the French do it though, topless and confident.

This casual nude, French cultural difference caused so much anxiety before I even left New York that I spoke about it with all my close friends. Actually I tortured my friends with a mantra, of-sorts saying, "Oh my God they bathe in the nude." Sincere, panicked-conversations were addressed over and over and over again, and then maybe just one more time.

How the hell am I going to go topless on the beach? How will I let these, *my 'bad-boys,'* out in the sun? They've never seen the sun! And by the way, me and *my bad-boys*, we're A-OK with that-- they have no need to see the sun.

And the French women all have the body shape of your average twelve year-old girl, with tiny-tits. I have D-cups! Add to that, as if I need to, I've been exposed to the sun for a while now and the rest of my body is very tan, leaving my boobs looking more than extreme-white. Severely white, bright and never-ever touched by the sun, might begin to express just how white they really are. I've got major contrast going on here which, if possible, make my boobs look even bigger. Minimally they say, 'We've never been in the sun before, look-at-us, look-at-us!'

I've managed to dodge this boob-bullet the past few weeks because since I have been in France, it has been chilly and rainy-thank God! I know I am the only person who is actually happy that the weather sucks. *My bad-boys* and I felt safe behind our fleece sweater, inside, under-cover, exactly where they were born and raised and meant to be. And yes, I know most gals call their boobs 'the twins' or 'the girls' mine aren't like that; they are simply best described as *My bad-boys* or *The Bad-boys*; for that-- you'll have to take my word.

But the anxiety, just the wait is enough to do me in. Oy, the mere thought of it haunts me and my boobs. This huge D-cup deadline, just sits there and waits. I feel it as it looms in the background, a heavy, weighty, overwhelming sense of doom. I am telling you, there's plenty of anxiety out there and remember, this is before Xanex was prescribed by knowing doctors or found everywhere or sold in gum-ball machines, so I have to tough it out. And the thing is there's no one on this side of the Atlantic that I can possibly talk to about this who could understand. I need a pinch-hitter shrink. I left all my non-boob-sun-bathing friends back in The States. My new Frenchie friends, they couldn't possibly get it. They have these teeny tiny tits that are wildly tan and bursting to get back out there into the French sunshine, and mine aren't and I don't.

So here is the thing, I'm thinking I cannot just go out there and do this. I mean, I need some kind of preparation or something, maybe even a dress rehearsal. Really, I suppose an un-dress rehearsal is more accurate. I need to find a way to get comfortable with this, or at least get to a point where I won't throw-up at the mere thought of it.

So while Philippe is at work, I decide to go for a practice run, it is one of the first semi-nice days in a long while. And in fact, I think it's a damned-good idea too. I went to the beach were everyone hangs out surfing, it's called Verte Bois and it's about a mile walk from our home. There are two ways you can get to the beach. One is a road that circles around and you can actually see the dunes from the road where you park. The other way is a more enchanting route. There is a long path you can walk or ride your bike on, through an extensive pine forest that this part of the Island is known for. The scent of the pine studded greenery is delightful and muffles the sound of the beach and narrows your vision before you get to the sand-dunes. It also is fresh and shaded and delicious in every way. Once you're past the Forét des Saumonards the landscape opens before you and you see blue skies, surfers and sand.

When you get off the path you can go to the left towards the cabin where they store their surfboards and hang out; that would be everyone we know, or you can go to the right, where it is less crowded and void of anyone I would know. I take my practice-walk through the pine-path and purposefully decide to go to the right. I walk far down the beach where very few people are strolling around. Believe me, one person every hour is more than I'm used to flashing *the bad-boys* at, so that will be plenty, even though it will be basically void of people.

Phew… it's empty. Just me… the sand, the pine trees in the background and one big bathing suit to roll down. Here, if you were a one-piece you roll the top down, and for a two piece you simply pop the top off! Some stores even sell two-pieces but-without the top. Just the bikini bottom- technically I suppose a one-piece but I digress. Me, I have a traditional one-piece so I know I need to just roll it down and quickly apply # 50 as I do not want to burn *the bad-boys*. Whoa sunburn, that is an image that is scary and could actually put quite a damper on my holiday right? Truth be told, I have already applied many layers of Coppertone back at the house... a preemptive strike. I'm not that much of a risk-taker. Hey, maybe I should just head home and wash the floors or something.

OK anyway, I manage to keep my ass on the beach, which is pretty good. Now for *the bad-boy* reveal moment... it's all about practice, the reason for my excursion today... the roll-down. No-one is insight. Not one person for as far as my eyes can see. So getting my top off is in-a-way, a technicality. Three-two-one, I get my top off and I lie down and I confirm, no humans in sight. I am so grateful, no-one is around. Practice points for me; me, and the air, the sand and the sun and my two very large, very white boobs. Everyone just needs to get used to it.

My boobs are in shock from so much air, the air is probably in shock from so much boob. I am astounded. I am very alone on the beach, yet all exposed in a public place. Despite the shock and anxiety, we all make it through. Yes, I see this as a team sport.

I can hear the old emergency broadcasting announcement in my head. "This is a test of the emergency broadcasting system, if this were a real emergency Judy's boobs would not be basking in the French sun." OH crap, all right already, I tell myself to keep my focus, after all this is just a test for me and my boobs. It isn't so much a matter of--can we get used to this, but how quickly? Are we sure Xanex isn't prescribed on this side of the Atlantic yet?

I squiggle my butt a little bit deeper into the sand to get comfortable and perhaps to sink a little lower from view. I can hear my every thought pounding in my head. 'Hmmm' .... I think, 'this isn't too bad... I can handle this, silly Americans, silly me; after all, it's just a body. Why are we so damned prudish?' A moment or two later, I'm thinking, 'OK girl, not bad, you are doing well on the test, you are reasonably calm and pretty darned cool too.' I mean really cool. Let's face it – this is the height of coolness in my life or at least for this week. And after all that fuss... and now I feel *OK*, a vast improvement from where I expected myself to be.

'Hey you know what, this is kind-of-nice and after all this worry, liberating. Just think... it might be nice to have tanned boobs.' I dare to open my eyes to look at my boobs, as if to confirm they are indeed out in the sun and to verify that they will ultimately have a chance and being tan. I think, clearly I am at least three weeks away from being a tan goddess. I try to examine them without staring and so I try to casually look down to see if they've been cooked or not. Nope, all seems good down there. The #50 sun block is holding out, as is my anxiety. Thank God, because the thought of re-applying sun block on my boobs in a public setting, is, well, it isn't happening that's for sure. Technically I never thought much beyond getting to the beach and exposing my boobs. My plan was very short sighted. My strategy was just to practice getting *my bad-boys* out in the sun, I never even thought about what might happen next.

Definitely, not applying sun-block- nope, not happening and way beyond my capabilities at this point. Rome wasn't built in a day and my large-white-never-have-been-in-the-sun-boobs have been challenged enough today. Let's face it I'm still in the early moments of day one and counting; I'd say if I had to stop right now to give a self-evaluation-- I succeeded beyond my wildest dreams. And indeed, my strangest nightmares.

Only a few random people stroll by and I manage not to blush. Or if I do, I am grateful for the tan/sunburn on my face that hopefully hides my nervousness. Tomorrow is the real test anyway... I'll be with Philippe and many of his friends. Worse yet, it's Sunday and everyone has the day off! Every cute surfer with their adorable girlfriend will be here...OH MY GOD.

I privately pray for rain. I try to imagine it being the worst summer for weather with the most rain France has ever seen. I can feel myself wishing that I could turn on *The Today Show* and hear Al Roker beam, "Rain, rain, rain all over the coast of France where Judy is… so no scattered boobies tomorrow" but I know that- as much as I wish it so… clearly, that isn't likely.

You'd think I could explain my anxiety to Philippe, try to articulate my feelings to the man I am falling in love with… but I can't. Basically the problem is he's so, so ….well, French. How could he understand? He's genetically pre-disposed to NOT being able to understand. He was born in a breast-exposed, boob-beach-loving country… it's not his fault.

So with the sun beaming in the sky and sand stuck to my boobs, I know I have accomplished my mission today. I declare, 'One giant step for my boobs and one super-giant step for American woman-boob-kind. Not to mention Coppertone #50.'

I try to act casual that night when Philippe notices a slight tan. "Oh yeah," I say, demure as can be, "finally we had nice weather today, so I hit the beach." He grins, happy about the rain finally ending, completely unaware, oblivious to my incredible accomplishment. He cheerfully reminds me that he has the day off tomorrow and that we're supposed to have good weather too, "A perfect beach-day." Great. I can hardly wait.

Sunday, the mother of all Sundays comes… and we pack our bags to head to the beach. I tell myself an Academy Award is at stake and I just have to play the part, the one I have rehearsed for, the one I am ready to tackle and born to play. We work our way to the beach, we make that clear, very distinct left-hand turn I had so specifically and strategically avoided yesterday. I know we are headed down the beach and we will meet up with friends. And of course we do. Not just any friends, French friends who are all gorgeous, incredibly stunning size-two French friends, whose boobs have seen and bonded-with the sun their entire lives. They are tan, tiny and frickin' perky too. Great.

My D-cups sigh into my covered-chest, as we approach. Philippe leans down and kisses his friends hello. This is, after all, the first time he has seen them today. And he is just following the well-established social kissing-greeting rules.

'OH MY GOD, OH MY GOD, OH MY GOD!!! I forgot about the kissing! How could I forget about kissing?' My chapped lips and I begin to wonder, *my bad-boys* start to panic. I was so damned obsessed with the boob thing I forgot that there would be kissing too. I really, really, really needed a few more days of rehearsal. I am definitely not ready for all of this!

My inner voice speaks loudly at times. All I can hear is, 'AHHHHHHHHH' then I try to calm and comfort myself and repeat in my head, 'FORGET ABOUT KISSING. One step at a time... you can do it, you have to do it!'

I haven't seen these people yet today either but I am thinking, 'You gorgeous people all have your damned cute little boobs out and about in the breeze; I'm not kissing you four times!' So I pull a stupid American trick; I tell myself this is a great fall-back position that I can still manage since I've only been here a brief while- knowing full-well, it isn't so. I demonstrate a complete lack of manners plus less-than-zero etiquette and I flash a big generic American-style group wave that I know damned well is against all greeting rules and I sit down on my towel.

I can hear the thoughts pounding in my brain. I think, be casual, cool, just keep talking and talking and talking and organizing your towel for a minute... but of course my French sucks, so what can I say other than a quick hello. (Really, regretting my current vocabulary count of fifty-three words.) 'Damn it, just lie down then roll the frickin' bathing suit down.' I just need to get that first moment behind me. I need a quantum leap. I picture myself, jumping off of a cliff. Once I step over the edge, I know I will be propelled by gravity.

I organize and straighten my towel one last time, perfectly tucking the corner under a neat pile of sand. And then just two, maybe three last towel corrections. I decide to place my Coppertone on the edge of my towel; I take my book out of my backpack and I even fold every piece of clothing in a precise manner and place it ever-so neatly inside my sack. In my entire lifetime my beach towel and clothing have never been so perfectly taken care of.

Remember, they have NEVER seen boobs as big as mine in all of France and I can guarantee no-one on the entire continent has seen boobs as WHITE, as mine - ever. OK, I attempt to sooth myself.... just stretch out, lie down and do it.

I should mention in all fairness that you really do have a choice; you can leave your top on, if you want to. Something I contemplate at this very moment. If you do leave your top on however, you will be the one out of a million that does, and you'll get even more attention than if you don't. So there is a choice, be the only person on the French Coast-line with your top on... or get it over with and let *the bad-boys* run free. It doesn't seem like much of a choice to me. No, I want to be cool, I am in France I am going to be cool, cool, French, normal French, topless French, even if it kills me.

I literally have a soundtrack with a strange male announcer voice-over banging around my brain at this point. 'OK, all systems go, we are ready for top-roll down, in five-four-three-two-one; blast-off.' The top is being rolled down. No-one is looking. Well, how would I know? My eyes are of course are glued shut. I just want to block out the world. I keep giving myself positive affirmations.

After a few minutes, I manage to block out the people around me, it's incredible. My boobs seem to suddenly have superhero blocking-out powers that I was unaware of. Thank God! Super D-cup boobs, able to leap tall buildings in a single bound, able to block out cute French people that scurry around us, this is magic I tell you. Finally and un-expectantly, a brief glimpse at what life must be like as a super-hero. (Note to self: Marvel Comics should really investigate the boob-baring super-hero concept.)

After a while, I allow my mind to focus on others. I allow my eyes to open and I try my best to be normal. The guys get up to surf and of course I had seen this before, they just pull their bathing suits right off and then slap on their wetsuits. Likewise, people often change from their street clothes into their swim gear without any indication that they might be intimidated, insecure or vulnerable. They seem unabashedly unashamed-- amazing.

Today I take a little bit of solace in this, that everyone is exposed at some point in the day. But I really don't want to see that either. That is way too much nude-penis action; I mean random, unknown penises everywhere. Well-frankly- this isn't doing anything to calm my nerves today. I have enough to think about... me, nude-er-ella. Besides, I think my initial estimate of three– weeks-to-tan-boobs was way off, *these bad-boys* could take months to get tan and even longer before they are accustomed to the breeze. God help me but I've got my big-white-bad-ass-American boobs, OUT, and by *OUT*, I mean... so far out. Yup, *the bad-boys* have relocated... they are now officially outside, amongst the cute Frenchies, out for the entire universe to see. The fact that they are so, oh-so white, means that most-likely they can be seen from space too, but this is a fact, I have yet to verify. I should check with NASA.

I can feel my thoughts break away and quickly spiral into a frenzy of sorts. Where'd my super-hero powers disappear to? My life as a super-hero was very short-lived, indeed. 'OK – calm...quiet the mind, after all, it's a day at the beach. Settle in and it will be over soon.' I even attempt to look around for a moment or two. Focus on the good stuff. 'Hmm,' I say to myself, 'Nice day, beautiful beach and beautiful people.'

I am, if truth be told, in an odd way, almost proud to have my first public-beach-boob, moment over. Actually I'm swollen with pride, satisfied at my accomplishment. I'm thinking --damn the expensive phone bill, I'm calling one of my friends tonight. This is a $40 dollar story, if ever I had one. At the same time I am 'doing it' I am sort of having an out-of-body experience. You know, when you see yourself from above, like you are floating outside of yourself. I embrace that concept. I am all too happy to be out of my body.

Moments later I look down the beach and I see two of Philippe's friends, Kristoff and Gregory. They are approaching from a distance. They are two typical French men, or typical to the Island anyway. Friendly, surfer types, who are super cute, adorable actually, they would be considered hotties by North American standards. They have both been so nice to me, so friendly. And here they come and I am lying here half nude.

'It's OK', I try to remind myself, 'They are French, and they do this all the time.' Suddenly I remember... shit; I haven't seen them yet today either. Crap, Crap, Shit! This of course means that I haven't kissed them hello yet. 'No way are they going to kiss me, I'm topless.'

They are now steps away, I am silently freaking out. Sure enough, in slow-motion, at least in my memory, Kristoff leans down towards my perfectly laid out towel, kisses me, first to the right, *kiss*, then to the left, *kiss*, and says, "Bonjour, Ca va?! I can't remember if I said Ca va or threw up... but I think I muttered something. Gregory (Hottie number two) is now coming over, same thing happens... it is as if I am actually wearing clothes and not secretly screaming inside my mind. *Kiss* to the right, to the left. The only thing I am grateful for is that they are Island-guys, so it was a standard-two-kiss event; thank God, thank Jesus, thank Budda, Allah and Moses- it wasn't four kisses. That'll come later at some pro-boob-beach tournament no doubt, probably tomorrow. All I can think is that I went further with these guys then I have with more than most men I ever dated! Me and my super-hero boobs, my American girlfriends would be proud.

Add to that, tonight I am going to sit across from these people and eat dinner with them, holding the fork and knife in a proper manner, like nothing ever happened. And the only one who gets how damned funny and bizarre this is, is me. It's a lonely thought.

Before I fall asleep, cozy at night with my big-day (My big boob-Sunday) behind me, I started to think; what happens when you get to the beach and there are twenty-three people there that you are friendly with, and you haven't seen them earlier in the day, all with their boobs and penises out and about? You guessed it- based on the average three-kiss approach, I'd have sixty-nine kisses. That is a visual that puts one big-ass grin on my face as I try to doze off into sleep. I giggle a little into the pillow, immature as I am. I am quite certain that that last thought will deliver some seriously funny dreams.

Friday in France

Chapter 10: A NICE Jewish Girl

What lies behind us and what lies before us are tiny matters compared to what lies within us. ~Ralph Waldo Emerson

One's destination is never a place, but a new way of seeing things. ~ Henry Miller

All I keep thinking is, how did a nice Jewish girl like me get to a place like this? I'm hanging out (literally) with people on the beach with our bathing suits half off. I'm kissing everyone, in truth, anyone who comes within two feet of me, men, women, children... Hmmm, come to think about it, what am I complaining about?

It's just that, as an American, and as a Jewish gal at that, I've been trained. Pre-programmed to be a particular someone, if you will-- someone who will lead a specific life style. It isn't preordained or anything and I certainly do not qualify as a JAP

(On any planet) which maybe the most irritating version of what some might think I should be. It is more that like this; I've been raised to be an educated, giving, caring, upstanding member of society, someone who contributes with whatever talents I have. I've been raised to be the best I can be, to work hard, study hard and to use whatever I gain from my studies to make my contribution to the planet. To volunteer, give back, behave, be a good girl- wherever I live.

Also, I feel now for the first time in my life, that I've been raised in a prudish society. I'm not a prude, really I'm not, but in a public, exposed-nude-way I guess I've discovered that I am. The idea of being comfortable or uncomfortable with my body, what's up with that? I'm almost surprised to even find out that I have an issue, because at home, I don't. Back home though, boobs are not public property.

Where do you learn that brazen self-confidence? And I just don't mean being able to be publicly nude. Women in France barely wear any make-up if at all. Their skin magically glows without it. The walk with an air of confidence, whether or not they are actually attractive they exude self-assurance. They age gracefully and magnificently too. The inner confidence no doubt feeds the way they radiate poise and polish. They wear simple clothes and make a pair of jeans and a white t-shirt look like a stunning, coordinated outfit.

I went to SUNY New Paltz, a state university near New York City, believe me, they didn't offer courses on that type of confidence there! Nope, no class is going to do it for you. It's in the air. It's in the media, it's in – well how the hell would I know? Because whatever 'it' is, it hasn't been anywhere that I've even been, until now. It's a cultural mindset in which most American women do not participate. It might even be beyond a cultural mindset that is gender specific and that is not a tangible world for my little American brain.

Mind you, New York women are fashionable, stylish and have a certain air about them. We also remain primarily covered, so having poise and grace might be easier with your shirt on!

Even in the city that never sleeps, it was so much more conservative than here, really. I smirk to myself ... I'm a mini-skirt gal. Gee-wiz, how open and hip and courageous of me; I show my legs, 'how edgy' but really, I do not show off my boobs. I barely wear anything that shows cleavage. Hell, in my New York City wardrobe I tend to wear a black shirt with some kind of little jacket over top. I'd sport a little bolero number, or a blazer, something to keep *the bad-boys* close to me and out of the public view.

Here, on Olerón, it's more sophisticated and body comfortable than the biggest most progressive cities in The U.S. And when looking around the Island beaches you can see that Grandmas and twelve year-olds sit side by side on the beach, boobs flapping in the breeze, with no real care, no thought to it. It was just how it is.

OK so having the largest boobs on this side of the Atlantic is my problem. As a Jewish girl, that is pretty common; the big boob part, I mean. I know I should get over this boob thing but it really is such a paradigm shift. It really illustrates so perfectly one of the main differences between our culture and theirs.

One day I remember our friend Eric was with us strolling on the beach, and he said (In French of course, but I must translate) "Wow, lots of nice boobs out today." I almost fell over. I mean, are they or aren't they casual about it? Is it natural or unnatural for them to see the boob-fest on their beaches? It seems that it is actually a bit of both. They appreciate the boobs, being out and especially the beautiful ones, but they aren't shy or weird about it. I guess that is my best tit-assessment I can make.

The thing is, nice Jewish Girls don't normally have to make tit assessments. Nice Jewish girls don't leave their successful careers behind to go have an adventure in France either. Really, I was raised to be a nice, smart person, perhaps one that would go on to have a career, or raise a family. So leaving a successful career behind wasn't at all what anyone had planned for me... even me.

For that matter, nice Jewish girls date doctors and lawyers and CPAs and a random architect perhaps, but never, ever date French surfers, let alone, French surfers with no life ambitions. Is that redundant?

But you know what, the funniest thing happened on the way to a full-body tan. I got used to it. I got my Jewish, big-D-cup-boobs, tanned, and I liked it. There was a freedom hidden in that tan. It was kind of sexy and it was certainly new and different for me.

For as covered and fast as I was in New York, I was now equally exposed and slow on the Island. And perhaps the most important aspect of it all was that within weeks it did become a natural state of being. My shyness lifted. I didn't care anymore. I was just there. No inner-dialogue, no panic, no unease, just stillness, calm and confidence in my nakedness.

Maybe you think this shouldn't be considered a phenomenon, a miracle of sorts or that it shouldn't replace any of the seven wonders either. But to be fair to me and my boob-accomplishment, it isn't something that can be easily measured. I can tell you this is beyond a phenomenon in my humble assessment; oddly enough, eventually it felt natural, free, normal and frankly, fabulous.

Everything with my boobs and the public sun started to seem way-more normal in just a few short weeks from my original un-dress rehearsal; as did the pace I was now living, well almost, that one might take a while. Once they were tanned, I definitely felt like I blended in a bit more and that's very important to me. Once I started to take advantage of the slow pace of life, I could start to adjust to my new 'news-free-self' as well. And I am sure that not feeling weird about it on the inside helped me bare my outsides too- at any speed.

Still, a few scattered boob-sun-bathing highlights that did take place later on that summer come to mind. I remember after I had been there for a few days Philippe announced that his parents would be coming down for a three week visit and staying in a house around the corner. WHAT? OK for sure I was keeping my top on when we were all on the beach together! Right? I mean, well who cares what their culture said about it, there was no-way, and no-how I could 'hang with them.'

As an aside, neither of them really spoke a word of English, and Philippe was working so I would go to visit them and we would get the dictionary out and try to talk. I remember being on the beach together using sticks to draw in the sand; making our own version of Pictionary on the beach, just to try to understand each other. (All fully dressed, thank you.) They spoke less English than anybody else I'd met thus far, probably because they were part of a different generation. It could easily take thirty minutes to communicate some mundane stupid thought. But it was worth it. Paule and Firmin, Philippe's parents, were charming. I just wasn't used to meeting parents so soon. Ah what the hell. As long as it takes place in another language on another continent, and my boobs are behind closed clothes, it can't possibly really count, right?

When Philippe's folks would happen along the beach and I would run into them while I was hanging out (literally) with friends, they thought it was hilarious (As did my friends) that I would scramble to cover-up. Covering up was the only thing to do... clearly, because not –doing so, well, that that would be crossing some line I am unwilling to cross. I do not need to sit with my boyfriend's parents, my potential future Mother and Father-in-law with *my bad-boys* out-and-about. I don't need to feel that 'evolved' either.

Another boob moment close-call (So to speak) was with a friend of mine, Daniel, from Paris (A four-kiss guy) who used to perform 'pseudo-chiropractic' techniques on me (As I requested.) I missed my chiropractor guy on The Upper East Side- 60th and 3rd Ave. Daniel was a full-time nudist, none of this wetsuit on and off thing for him. He just 'hung out' on the beach with his wife and son and his penis... all the time.

One day Daniel volunteered to crack my back on the beach. For this event, I decided to pull my bathing suit top up, come on... even for boobs with super-hero powers, this is a bit much. Needless to say, I handed him a towel too. And we both laughed, so you see the French <u>do</u> see the nakedness but, I guess they are just all right with it.

Later that summer, my friends Patty and Mary came to visit. These are the very same New York City friends who I confided in before my departure. Confided, complained to, and freaked out to about how I was going to go topless in France. These are the same friends who knew just how much I didn't want my boobs to come out in public. There I was, warning them before they arrived… "Listen" I kind-of yapped, "There are going to be boobs out everywhere… as far as the eye can see, and uhm, mine included… just wanted to give you a head's up on that!" I was the epitome of the evolved traveler, who had taken the French culture to heart, well, at least all the way to my chest.

One more 'little note' for now on this topic; I think the surfer guys have it kind of rough too. I mean the water in the Atlantic is COLD, and they have to undress, in and out of their wetsuit. PUBLIC undressing after cold water is tough on the male ego. OH sure the Frenchies manage to hide their concerns pretty well, but come on, any man whose penis is shrunk to half its size, can't be HAPPY about bringing Mr. Happy out in public, circumcised or not!

I got used to everybody whipping off their clothes… it was as natural as, being nude could be. I did find applying sun block and swatting away bugs from certain body parts a bit odd even with many months of experience… but that was OK. I mean you can take the gal out of America but you can never take ALL of the America out of the gal.

Chapter 11: The Art of Food Worship

I will not eat oysters. I want my food dead. Not sick, not wounded: dead. ~ Woody Allen

If you reject the food, ignore the customs, fear the religion and avoid the people, you might better stay at home. ~ James Michener

Learning the basics about the French culture definitely would mean including cracking the food-code. I mean, I want to fit in and I want to absorb my time here, and I want to really figure it all out. You can't really begin to do that without taking a hard look at the differences in the way they eat and even the way they look at food.

Most people think that the French have elevated food well beyond a true art form. Perhaps that is correct, but I would say it has taken on a power greater than that. It is a religion. No, more than that... it is a way of life... it sustains life and in fact, makes life worth living.

I believe, that when Moses was up on Mt. Sinai talking to a burning bush and receiving The Ten Commandments, I think some French-dude (Most likely named Philippe... no, Jean-Claude) was on the other side of the mountain receiving The Ten Commandments of Cooking. These laws were carved into a big wheel of Brie.

This is how the French have mastered the paradox of all paradoxes: more fat inside food, least amount of body-fat per capita and on the planet. They are the skinniest, non-third-world country, to say the least.

Here goes:

Thou shall use crème recklessly.

Thou shall overuse butter.

Thou shall eat brains, livers, and snails.

Thou shall create a pâté out of every imaginable animal part.

Thou shall not covet thy neighbor's food, and always say 'bon appetite' to any person you see eating.

Thou shall consume an apéritif prior to every meal, in order to open the taste buds and begin the celebration of eating.

Thou shall consume wine; red, and white or rose with every meal that takes place after 12pm.

Bread, shall be treated as the only other God, please carry under your armpit so it can be located close to your heart.

Thou shall offer a *prix fixe* menu at every restaurant (Fixed priced meal), with a minimum of three courses.

Thou shall have a patisserie on every street corner.

Then Jean-Claude took the commandments (Not easy to carry through the desert as they were carved into a big wheel of Brie) and headed east towards France. Voila, the holy land, the land that worshipped food had its laws and privileges. So the Israelis got God's word and the right to eat endless falafels with humus (Both good, but cannot hold a candle to a crêpe); and the French, the French got the world of fine food and wine. Not too shabby.

Me, being a mere American, with taste-buds that have experienced a good pasta or two, matzo ball soup for a touch of the exotic … was lost in this culture. It isn't that I couldn't worship food; I just couldn't do it like they did.

I am a nice Jewish Girl after all, and we do our share of food worship, it is just more like, eat, eat, eat instead of taste, taste, taste. We love food, love to over eat it for every occasion. Celebration equals food. Sad equals food. Stressed equals food. Bored equals food. Everything… equals food.

One of the scariest Jewish customs is after a Bris (When they cut the tip of the baby boy's penis off-AKA-circumcision) then everyone gathers together and, what do we do? We eat, because celebrating life is about eating.

With the French, it is never the size of the dish, it is always about how glorious it tastes. What elements, what qualities does it have and can you find in the dish? You'll hear men, women and children around a table talk about the food. Closely evaluating it, they actually examine it, and enjoy every bite of it. They'll say things like, 'Taste the vanilla, the raspberry, a hint of dill' whatever they find and detect in each bite, then they rejoice over it, analyze it and taste it some more.

'Notice the hint of earth and berries.' 'I love the way it reveals itself and at the end I find that the back of the mouth is delighted with a splash of licorice.' 'The slight suggestion of citrus is highlighted by the compliment from the crème.'

What I do not understand is how the hell, do they keep their figures? The average women there is a size two (Max!) The FDA would be shocked to know that they gobble saturated fats in the form of crème, butter, sausages, pâté, cheese... did I mention crème? Someone needs to help me, a helpless American who had a good twenty pounds to lose. I need to find some guidance.

There I am eating salads, with the dressing on the side of course. This is a concept that not one French waiter has managed to really understand. I look over my shoulder at the petite men and women and there they are, eating pizza topped with cheese, crème and sausages for their first course! Of course they pour oil on top to add flavor, 'You have to have oil!' Followed by the second course, that was made of crème, poured over some meat, with potatoes and some bread to slop up any remaining crème. Oh sure, they drink red wine, big shit! I'll drink wine too- no problem, start pouring. I've been drinking wine (tequila, vodka etc.) for years now, but I still have to pull my weight at the gym and I still have to count frickin' calories!

The French say, looking down on us, 'but we walk though'. That may work against most Americans, but not me, not a New Yorker. I used to walk a minimum of three miles a day, closer to six without any effort, and then drag my cholesterol ridden body up four flights (186 steps) to my fourth floor walkup apartment. I got all that exercise every day just to get to work and around town. Then I'd hit the gym three times a week too, go figure.

Thanks to our American society, I had the FDA and the fat-free fad, etched deep into my mind. In France that was challenged with my ability to watch these guys!! The battle in my mind began and raged on; eat oil, don't eat oil, eat crème- don't eat crème, and so it went. Luckily I decided to basically work out three hours a day and eat a tomato for lunch... and I lost the weight I wanted to reasonably quickly, but not fast enough. I still had my big-ass boobs though.

When I say I am jealous, I am. When I say, it's not fair, it isn't! To say I began some undercover quest to unlock the French Food secret was an understatement. I watched, I looked, and I listened, I spied, I scouted, I examined menus, I looked for patterns, I did it all. I prayed with a tiny-winy voice, I want to eat cheese too!

Dear French Food God,

I promise to follow The Ten Commandments of Cooking. I promise to worship every morsel. I will even commit to eating brain pâté, (someday) and drinking Pastís and I will even swear that I will carry bread under my arm pit, if that is what it takes to show my devotion. I want to eat cheese for dessert (Oh yes I will!) If only you'll allow me to wear a size two without effort! I noticed that exercise is not mentioned within The Ten Commandments of Cooking, I just want to understand HOW? How can it be? Oh, French Food God, I need so much faith, and yet I challenge the belief system. It's not that I don't want to believe, OH HOW I WANT TO BELIEVE. Believe me.

Help me, for I am American, and we do non-fat or sugar free or Big-Macs until we are obese... I do not know from your rules, as I come from the land of high-cholesterol even though you and I both know that the Frenchies really should have that title! I simply beg for your guidance and understanding. Repeat, beg. I have a great hunger to comprehend. With an undying thirst to learn your ways, I am at your mercy. I plead for your assistance.

Most sincerely,

The diet-challenged, yet dedicated-American

And there it is, I'm not proud, I'm just tired. I've prayed to the French Food God and now I will try to think like a French person, be a French food person.

Here goes: I order pizza, it comes to me; you know one of those thin crust pizzas, OK good. Wait, what is that floating in the middle- CRÈME? On PIZZA? I can't do that, I don't even want to do that. But what if the French Food God thinks my prayers are insincere? I eat the outer edges, and pretend to save the best for last.

I'm going to be the size of 6th Avenue if I eat like this. But what if the French Food God knows all- sees all?

Next day: I order a salad- good right? It comes with a poached egg on top of toast, then lettuce, tomatoes, pears, smoked ham and some weird-ass cheese all over it. It is smothered in dressing. Not only is this a calorie buster, who the hell wants to waste calories on this crap? But, I mumble 'Bon appetite' to my dinner companion and I pick through, digging out any vegetable I can find. Secretly hoping that a dog will happen on by and I can pass it off to him.

This may sound odd but indeed dogs and restaurants do go together in France. Yup, they do allow their pooches in restaurants. At first I was shocked, but it is very French. They actually treat their dogs better than they do most tourists! But alas, at this exact moment, not one dog in sight.

The apéritif concept is a good one. Great, actually. Have a nice drink before your meal. Champagne, a Kír, a beer, a Pastís. A lot of the apéritif choices are ones that don't work for me, but I managed my way around it. Again, I wonder if the French Food God will be angry with my lack of adventure... I was served all sorts of Pinauds which takes some getting used to; it's a specific apéritif from the region made out of a mixture between cognac and the poor wine grapes that come from the Island itself... very sweet, kind of Manischewitz Wine like. And of course there are beers, each served in its designated brand-labeled glass, which they sometimes mix with lemonade or whatever they concoct. I said "YUM YUM" out loud in case the FFG (French Food God) is watching over me. One of the funny things the French do, is they serve a snack along with the apéritif. What is funny about it is the size, or lack there-of. They'll serve a bag of twenty chips to five people. Everyone has like four chips. Done, OK maybe right there, right there is a diet secret I've uncovered. They also serve olives as a snack instead of pretzels, now that is really, my kind of country!

Once you've had a few before dinner, your appetite is definitely open and you can further enjoy the meal. Then they start uncorking the wine... and lots of it. I have no problem with that! My only issue is that I know nothing about wine. Well, all right, here's what I know:

Red, (Check) white (Check) after that, I'm out, and I've got nothing!

The thing about wine and French people is this; if food is their religion than wine is undoubtedly their God, or at least a high-priest.

They don't get down on their knees and pray exactly, but they are obsessed with it. They critique, comment, evaluate and admire wine as if the world revolves around it. Well, the French world actually does revolve around it, so that kind of makes sense. The thing is, if you are me, and you are sitting amongst those that are over examining their glass of wine... you have nothing to add to the conversation. And the French don't let you simply sit and listen, maybe learn a little. They would call me out, usually first, before anyone else, "Judith, what do you think about the wine?"

Inside, I would answer, "It's wet, and red, and I am confident about that." Out loud I would mumble "I don't know, it's nice, I like it," add to that, this was usually in my bad-ass French... well, I didn't impress anyone. The kind of comments they are looking for are related to the wine's inner qualities; is it earthy, woody, piney, fruity, leathery, fresh, light, heavy, dark, what spices can you sense... what flavors are the most subtle? Can you tell what kind of barrel it has been kept in? Do you know if the roots ran-deep looking for water? Or was it in a region that had too much sun that year? Can you even tell the difference between an area that had drought or too much rain? Can you tell me what citrus fruit you taste? And can you tell me the order of the flavors that you taste; what reveals itself first? Do you taste the earth? Can you savor the earth? Do you taste the cassis? Does it open in the front of your mouth or in the back and how long does it take to do all of that?

And be specific please. They need to know if it was a good year or, is it similar to another. This is basic crap for them. I can't remember nearly enough of what was said as they looked at it longingly and appraised it. It was so outside of my awareness and ability as a wine taster. Usually I would say, "C'est super," it's good or something equally as inane, and they would follow up with; "It is verte, (green) too young, not good at all'. So what are asking me for in the first place if you know the answer? I want to travel back in time and take a wine-tasting class so I can at least fake it.

What I do know is, it kept my belly warm, the food digesting, and maybe just maybe, aided in lowering my cholesterol. I can say, it lowered my inhibitions and made me feel more comfortable hacking my way along some intense conversation in French. And on occasion I allowed it to lower my desire to stay on my diet. But other than that, I got nothing. I love wine, and I adore the fact that the French have a real love affair with it. I just felt like I was a bit on the sidelines. Which is kind of awkward when it comes to a love-affair, I mean, being a third wheel in all isn't exactly the desired role to play. I guess I was a peeping-Tom enjoying the voyeuristic qualities of those in love. So I listened and tried to take mental notes. I was just so enamored with their genuine admiration of wine, that it made it difficult to concentrate and to really learn anything. Add to that, I was usually getting pretty buzzed tasting it over and over again, so then really… who cares?

I should note here that the French Food God did smile upon me, not for sucking the heads' of shrimps, or for eating cow-brain pâté but for, reveling in the joy and pleasure of enjoying every morsel. I went from a being a New Yorker who can easily multitask while eating; in fact I was someone who almost always multitasked while eating, and became someone who just, sat, for a long time and enjoyed each bite. I relished in each and every sip of wine, and enjoyed each loving word of admiration spoken along the way.

Friday in France

Chapter 12: Driving Around…

The one thing that unites all human beings, regardless of age, gender, religion, economic status or ethnic background, is that, deep down inside, we ALL believe that we are above average drivers.
~Dave Barry

Ah…so many pedestrians, so little time… ~ Robin Williams

Regardless of my American status or maybe because of it- I'm an over-analytical person and I can't stop myself from trying to figure things out here. Everything seems like a puzzle or a riddle to unfold, and after all- what else should I be doing with my time? I do think I finally understand why I keep seeing people push their cars into the gas station, instead of the old-fashioned, driving in method. Why? My first guess is because they close at 7pm. Some of them even close mid-day from 12-3pm as well. I honestly can't keep track. What I do know, is that I do not want to be one of those people, pushing the car, or the mini-van, into it.

So when I hit a full stop at the traffic light and looked at the gas-meter, which read, "Hey idiot, you're almost out of gas!" I was happy to learn that it was 6:55pm and I managed to get the mini-van into the gas station and out of an embarrassing situation. Luckily, I had been there before with Philippe so I sort-of understood that you actually have to drive past a booth, pay the attendant first then you head towards the pump. Another potential embarrassing moment averted!

The van looks more like a 1970's retro love-bug and its bright green color is rather obnoxious. It is a 1979 Renault, is truly the tiniest mini-van of all mini-vans I have ever seen. I tower over it and I am only 5'5". All the cars in this country resemble matchbox cars. Maybe a matchbox car pumped up on steroids. Regardless of their tiny stature they really make up for with speed. They are built that way perhaps to make it easier to zip in an out and around the tiny country roads. They blaze a trail at high speeds and take tight corners, with traffic lights and stop signs that sometimes pop out from behind the miniature buildings that are curbside.

To make things more interesting for me, the cars are not automatic. Since I haven't ever really driven stick, this took some getting used to. To make matters worse, the roads other than the Route National on the Island are about the size of an average American driveway. Not big enough to really handle two way traffic, even for baby-size cars. So sometimes you find that you have to hop-off the road in order to let someone else pass. The trick is, you can't see them coming and no one ever really knows who is supposed to hop-off, and who is to carry on. Delicate decision- making, without a doubt. At least to me, a new-bie.

There are also all sorts of traffic situations that are quite common to France but not really that common in The States. For example, there is the rond-point; a traffic circle with a cute-name that can go on and on, especially for those of us who do not know how to get off. I will admit that there's always plenty to look at; minimally pretty flowers of some sort or a well thought out landscaping in the center of the rond-point. You see the trick for me is that I didn't know where I was going; I can't read the signs either, so I need to take a few passes around so that I can sort-of figure out the information. Once I've had a chance to absorb it, then I can make a definitive decision. Clearly that complicates matters. So I'd go around several times, until I was confident that I had had taken-in the various signs and was reasonably confident in my exit choice and future direction. Then, I'd make my move. There were times when I felt like the traffic circle had become a home away from home.

Circling for quite a few laps, perhaps next-time I'll pack a sandwich, bring a book. Maybe I should fire-off a few postcards while I'm here. Minimally I should have a little bit of aspirin on hand, yeah that's a good plan because by the time I get the right of way I'll need them. I think carrying aspirin around, in France, is always an excellent strategy, especially if you are going to drive anywhere, anytime.

There is the push-your-car into the gas station, need for aspirin, and then there is another car push all together. I guess technically that would be more of a car pick-up rather than car-push. That is when a group of people, will actually pick up a car. A person will be located at each corner of the car then they'll simply lift it up, and move it, you know—carry it, into a tight parking space. This is a sight to see, and one you can happen upon more frequently than you'd think. It is really kind of cute actually and the first time I saw it, I couldn't believe it. I mean, I think in all my years of living in The U.S. I have never seen anyone park a car by picking it up. But the roads are so tiny and the parking spaces are so few that even the miniature sized cars sometimes has to be stuffed into their spaces. It doesn't really matter though, because when you look at any one of the narrow cobblestone streets in the center of any village, you could care less that parking maybe an issue; it's just so damned beautiful. BUT- Yeah, I say, carry aspirin in case the three friends who helped you pick up your car to park it- aren't around when you are ready *to get out* of that parking space. Undoubtedly, this is a good time to have aspirin or a spare group of friends, for that matter.

Then there is the push-to-start-your-car push. This I had seen on several occasions but I didn't get it, until I came face to face with the monster myself. Watching from a birds-eye-view I guess doesn't really count, because you're just a casual observer. It goes something like this, due to the mechanical fact that the cars are not automatic transmissions, you can push start them, when they need a little assistance. At least, that is what I have come to learn. This does require that you have several friends around; I'd say five is a good number. I would also say in hindsight that it is best, NOT to have your boyfriend be one of them. And I would double-down that statement if you happen to be a virgin to-pushing-your-car to start.

So there I am. I am told to get in the driver seat, and do something (I have no clue even to this day, what it was) and mess with the stick shift, maybe the clutch, maybe all at once. God only knows what because my vocabulary count has only increased to 117 words by now. Let's just say that my car-related or car-pushing related vocabulary is technically lacking. Regardless, the bottom line is after I do whatever it is I am supposed to do, then they will push the car to a reasonably fast speed, and somehow it will start. Anyway, all I remember is everyone yelling in French at me at the same time. And there I was struggling with the gears, until finally Philippe took over the driving part and I became a close-up observer, of The French Jump Start. In addition, I am now a close-up participant to feeling clueless, uneasy and insanely stupid.

Other alternatives to the tiny automobile hassles are of course walking and hitch hiking. Being from New York City – walking was totally cool by me. The island was actually the same size as Manhattan, more or less, but the little villages that dotted the landscape where really spread out. So walking, well, it had its limitations. I did walk to the beach though; I'd happily stroll through our neighbor's vineyard. But in our tiny village of Le Deux, there was really nothing else to walk to. There was this one weird-ass small grocery store-slash-bar of sorts that was at the second, of two stop-signs in our sleepy hamlet. This was the only commercial- anything in our town and it happened to be farmer-headquarters as well. Sometimes I would stop there to buy my nectarine or tomato lunch for the day- but the farmers in there used to stare at me and I, as the token American who preferred anonymity, sometimes found it just too much to manage. So even though I could --technically walk there, most times I used to walk past it.

The thing is, I do enjoy a long hike on occasion and so although the restaurant was over eighteen kilometers from our home, I did walk it a few times, just to say I did it. I would start by cutting through our neighbor's vineyard and then make my way on the windy road that connected our tiny town to the Route National. There was no sidewalk of course. I just walked on the side of the road for the most part. A town here, a village there and a lot of nothingness in-between. Now that's a dedicated walker. It took me well-over two hours. Ah, but those nights I felt like the French Food God would forgive any calorie consumption that might have followed.

There are other alternatives, biking; mopeds and motorcycles are all reasonable modes of transportation in France. The gas is so, so, so expensive that all of them make more sense than driving. In fact, you'll see old ladies driving motorcycles and young school kids riding around in packs on their mopeds. It is a way of life here, in this over-priced gasoline haven.

Philippe has an old BMW motorcycle that he loves. And he wants me to go for a ride with him, he has asked frequently. I am a little nervous, but I almost have to agree. He then tells me that the motorcycle doesn't really have a back seat. It is technically a one-seat motorcycle, with a fender, for my ass. And so we go for our first of several rides when it dawns on me, this mode of transport might actually be responsible for my not being able to easily get pregnant someday. In the reasonably close future it will be responsible for me losing all feeling in both butt cheeks--minimally. Either way, it is just a sign of my affection for Philippe that I will go for rides on his motorcycle in the future.

He does also offer me an occasional ride on the handlebars of his bicycle. This is a trick that I am unaccustomed to as well. In fact, this one really has me missing the taxis in New York City. But it's all so damned charming, and such an adventure and maybe because it happens in an alternate language, it has this foreign-film, art-house-flick quality to it. It seems like it should almost take place in black and white, just-to clearly express pure poetry of it all.

Chapter 13: Hoods or Sans Hood

Women are from stars, men are from penis. ~Van Bonta

My former life was mostly un-poetic. Everything was about multitasking. Especially at work. Although, I will admit that there were a few moments where all work seemed to stop. Where a conversation would simply take over and some kind of work-stoppage would follow. On one such day, back in the CNBC newsroom, a bunch of gals had gathered to chat about dating. Why we weren't gathering news is another story, but this is exactly the type of conversation that would force a break. Dating was an ongoing topic here and so we were all really comfortable with each other.

Someone yelled out, "Circumcised or uncircumcised?" no one really hesitated to answer and within moments it was clear

99%. Ok maybe 95% of the women there said without wavering, circumcised. Of course, this wasn't a formal survey as such. Regardless, I'm going with the 95% number, and that's a pretty overwhelming response. The remaining 5% just said they didn't care either way. It's kind of like four out of five dentists who recommend Trident.

A)   What is up with the 5th dentist?

B)   Do you really think the four dentists really care that much about what kind of sugar free gum you chew? Doubtful.

Do you think the circumcised is the sugarless version or the sugar-filled version? I don't know, I guess it is a matter of perspective. Do you look at a circumcised penis as missing something or one that isn't circumcised as having too much? Sometimes too much of a good thing ceases to be a good thing. That always depends on your personal perspective, a matter of personal opinion.

Anyway, four out of five dentists is what comes to my very analytical, very immature mind. Maybe I'm dodging the topic a bit because I am afraid that my parents are reading this. All I can picture is my Mom rolling her eyes and spitting my name out as she sucks on her teeth, saying, "Judy, really, did you have to go there?" Yes Mom, to be fair, I did.

So Ma, and Pa, do me a favor just skip ahead to the next chapter so my reader-buddies and I can 'talk amongst ourselves here.'

The fact is that even in New York City you can find your share of uncircumcised men... mostly foreigners. Most North Americans are cut. That's the plain, simple truth. So because of that, most North American women prefer that.

It's what we know, so we think it's what is best. It's like sugar free gum... if that is what you know... what you are used to... you really don't miss the sugar.

In France, I'd say 95% of the guys are uncircumcised. I think that's true in most of Europe, unless you are Jewish and cut for religious purposes. So I am not sure how great a Jewish population happens to have existed in France at that exact moment in time or now for that matter, but let's just say the majority of men are not. (Cut, that is). OK again, these numbers are not exact, and this isn't a scientific approach I am taking. Clearly I cannot vouch for each and every penis in France or in New York for that matter. Obviously, I did not get to see every single one of them for myself. So I am admittedly not an expert per se on dicks on either side of the Atlantic.

Can you imagine? There I am going door to door to run a survey? Frappe Frappe, (knock, knock) "Oui Monsieur, excusez moi Monsieur." Then I make an extreme bunch of gestures with my hands; I show the guy that he now needs to pull his pants down for this, the official government sponsored inspection. I flip it about in my left hand, casually. I mutter, "OK" And then I pull out my clipboard and check the appropriate box, I mark column B. Uncircumcised it is. I make a few general notes and I move on.

Stop for a moment and just appreciate that visual, would you please? Perhaps it would be easier to just walk along the beach and time it so that when men are slipping out of their wet bathing suits into their dry clothes I can simply happen on by. The thing is you'd have to really stare quite intently to make a verifiable judgment call on that. And then again, with the cold-water shrinkage factor, you'd really have to be quite fixated on it. No, I'm going to stick with my very unscientific approach and you'll just have to take my word for it, unless you decide to go door-to-door surveying on your own. Please send the results to me, if you do.

So if you like hoods, or if you don't like hoods, you should take that into consideration when traveling. As for my Philippe, you'll just have to guess. And it isn't any of your business quite frankly.

Bottom line is if 95% of the women surveyed answered that they didn't like the uncircumcised penises, went to France, they'd have damn few men to select from. And the other fact is, you don't really know until you 'get in there,' what you'll find. Kind of like a scratch off lottery ticket. It isn't one of those things you can kind-of know or even guess at in advance. But if you prefer the cut version

I'd say, vacation closer to home instead of l'ile d'Oléron, or if you are staying in New York City, stick with the American boys just to be safe.

And if you fall into the 5% category along with the rest of the 'I don't care girls,' you should find that 5th dentist that doesn't give a shit what kind of gum you chew, go for it and marry his ass.

Chapter 14: Love American Style

Everything should be made as simple as possible, but not simpler.
~Albert Einstein

Love doesn't make the world go 'round; love is what makes the ride worthwhile. ~Franklin P. Jones

Falling in love in France is not a bad way to go. For all of the past years in New York that were date-filled, but somehow lacking in romance, I say au revoir. Actually my New York dating had its share of excitement and cute men, no doubt, but it lacked that free-fall feeling, that total abandonment. It seemed that the people I was meeting there couldn't allow themselves to let go and fall in love... or maybe it was me. Either way, I can now toast to the lonely nights and the bad blind dates for which I feel are behind me. I drink to you, and I thank you for what I learned, and what it left me wanting more of.

With that, I can move on. France is truly a romantic place. Now, how's that for an original thought! It looks smells, tastes, sounds and feels romantic, funny enough, with or without a lover. OK, maybe, just maybe, the goose pâté lacks in romance for me but, everything else really smacks of it.

Since my last really serious boyfriend started in my college days and carried on for seven years (All keg filled younger-days,) this seems very different. I was actually having an affair in France…wow! How sophisticated of me, how *Cosmo Magazine* of me. How very adult, very adventurous, how amazing, how extreme and seriously sexy. Before my Philippe, it had been a while since I felt confident that my heart was safe to play and so I kept mine protected in a cocoon.

Now with my Philippe, there is safety here, it feels like a soft place to land…he wants to be in this. He allows himself to abandon all fear and embrace all hope… he wants to be in love and with one person. He isn't a typical French guy and he is light years from the typical New York guy who, after the third date thinks you want to have his child and starts looking for the exit.

No, my Philippe is ready for a relationship. *He* invited me to come live with him. Even though I agreed and I bought a four month ticket, in my mind I was going to spend a few weeks with him watch the entire thing unravel, completely fall-apart, and return to my natural state of singleness. First (Before my pre-planned NY return) I had it all worked out- that I'd travel through Europe make-out with cuties along the way, heal the wounds and then return back to New York City with some hilarious stories. But Philippe was so ready for me it caught me off-guard. In fact, he was actually able to be ready enough for both of us. He made it comfortable and easy to fall in love. This made for an uplifting and refreshing change. As mentioned, he's adorable, gorgeous by any standards. At 6'1" and with a surfer's body, he was easy on the eyes.

His eyes are hazel, with specks of blue-grey if I failed to highlight that before. His eyes actually have an extra kick, a special sparkle and they stand-out due to the contrast provided by his thick head of dark hair. He was a cutie alright, and he was a cutie in his manner. And the simple fact that he would lead the way; that he knew, that he felt easy about love, that he was there long before I, well, it made things way easier for me. Who knew? Who knew that I was a gal who had sadly, unknowingly, packed away her heart-strings during the long (Sometimes ridiculous) course of dating in New York the past few years? Not me.

Maybe because I had been in that long relationship in my younger years- I didn't get to know myself well enough, as an adult woman. Then of course, once I knew myself- I knew I didn't trust myself enough to truly connect to someone again. Now you see why the need for therapy.

For me, falling in love had a lot to do with letting down walls and pre-conceived notions. The fact that it took place in a foreign land and in a foreign language, with completely new and surreal circumstances, somehow made it easier for me as well. Almost as if it wasn't happening, so I could allow it to happen. I guess because it took place in such an unreal, bizarre way, I managed to magically and unknowingly let my guard down.

Looking back now I think it felt more like I was watching a made-for-TV-movie unfold. Actually, it felt more like an independent feature film and there I was, watching some characters on a screen. It was as if I had a bird's eye view and I was very removed from myself. Removed enough that I could let my emotions rise to the surface where it was safe to show them, in any language. I know that sounds odd but that- that is really the best way I can describe it.

At the very heart of the matter, it helped me open up. The fact that Philippe would pick wild flowers for me and insist that I ride with him on his bicycle handlebars on the way home from the beach, added to the sense that this was written in a movie script. He was so gentile and calm and he was reachable and very real. He didn't try or intend to be poetic, endearing and loving; he just is.

He is too simple, honest and caring to be a player or anything other than what he is- fabulous. Our romance was everything that NY wasn't.

I mean, my New York City dates would YELL for a taxi, or walk at a New York pace with me, but we never took a leisurely ride on a bike. And had someone asked me to ride on their handlebars through Central Park… well, it would have just been weird. Here, the backdrop of our romance, this lyrical, charming island set the pace, the peace and the playfulness of our relationship. Everything we are is all distinctly part of l'ile d'Oléron. Clearly I had made an attempt to get away from my New York City life, and this, well, this-was certainly not that.

We spent our days together in our tiny house that was clustered amongst others, in our little village of Le Deux. It was rather typical on the Island, and the stone-covered cottage was somewhere between 300-500 years old. No one knew exactly how old because to them 300 or 500 years- really was no big difference. Coming from The States where fifty years makes something an antique, you can imagine my intrigue. I believe that falling in love in France and in particular our village on the adorable Island of Oléron, in our teeny-tiny house made our romance a big romance, and it made it spectacular.

We used to keep the key to the house in the mailbox that was attached to the front door. OK—Time out. I didn't think that was charming at first either. At first- coming directly from Manhattan- I thought it was pure madness. Why not invite burglars and thieves directly into our home?

In New York City, those who live there, pride themselves on their locks and chains to protect themselves and their apartments. They buy stock in Medco-locks and buy bolts weekly to line their doors. I personally had bars on the windows and enough locks on my apartment door, to cover the security needs for any small country. But here, in Le Deux, we left the key for the door in the door. Actually the only reason why we even locked the door is because it wouldn't completely shut otherwise. Talk about charm, you can't make that stuff up.

We didn't have that many belongings so there wasn't that much to steal. In fact, we had no TV, no expensive jewelry, a very old stereo and really we had- nothing worth taking. We did have an exceptional amount of warmth, a great deal of chemistry and a certain enchanted energy that only a teeny-tiny compact 300-500 year old stone house could hold. And because we didn't have a lot of expensive toys we kept ourselves entertained otherwise. Brilliant.

Instead we read a lot, have a lot of great sex, or sometimes I paint and he fixes his BMW to pass the time. He likes to tinker with his surfboard, or fix up the bicycle and I like to watch the world go by. Our tiny house clearly had enough room for the important things.

I love, love, love, my absolutely adorable first French baby house. Yup, it was the smallest house in the world, probably the size of a NY studio or junior one bedroom or a standard size master-bathroom in middle-America. Did I mention it was tiny? Anyway, it had a garden wall lined with La Rose Tremiere (Hollyhocks) to the left of the driveway. The flowers sprouted up everywhere. They leapt up into the air overnight reaching eight-ten feet with ease. I swear these flowers had fantastic command as they would sprout in the crevices in the sidewalk where there was no soil at all. It looked a bit like what I imagined Oz to be like, and I loved it. Bright splashes of purple, red, pink and white would pop overnight and pour pure happiness from each pedal. Each region in France has an official flower; I didn't know that before I lived here. And now, I… we were lucky enough to live on the Island and to have Hollyhocks as our official flower. Talk about my good-fortune. When I tell you it was the perfect flower for this place, that's an understatement.

They lined up along the walls of the houses and lined the streets, giving the entire region this spectacular dream-like-air about it. These flowers pushed out from the stems, these thick stalks bounced alive overnight, and the blossoms unraveled themselves at a rapid pace; they were the only thing that seemed to move quickly here. They were in front of the grey-stone homes or in front of the white-washed homes with the dark blue, hunter green or light blue shutters and added a touch of color that helped to draw your eye up toward the sky.

We also had a fig-tree. Well, technically our neighbor on the other side of the flowered wall had a fig-tree that hung halfway into our garden. It provided great shade from the afternoon sun, as our baby-house was sans air-conditioning (As is most of France) and for my Philippe, it provided sweets; he adored figs and he'd jiggle the branches and make figs fall from the sky.

Philippe was the man that brought me to this garden. It made it even easier to love him... it... the Island and my new life, everything. For me, falling in love is something that in this case, I can't separate from the location. In fact, I fell madly in-love with the setting, this house which at some-point became my home, our home and our garden, long before I was willing to allow myself to fall in love with Philippe. The Island gave me the space and quiet that allowed me to fall in love; why would I want to separate any of that?

Of course, we did have our share of growing pains. Many of which derived from our language differences. In any relationship it is easy to be misunderstood, but when the two people involved speak two different languages, and can only muddle along in the other person's native tongue... trouble is usually not far behind. This inspired me to learn the language as fast as I could. My current vocabulary count has topped-off at 218 words.

On occasion, we'd discover that we could disagree for quite some time and then later find out that we were actually saying the same thing all-along. Over-all, we really didn't argue much though, with our scenic backdrop highlighted by our flowering walls and figs falling from the sky, we found little to fight about. We spent most of our time looking lovingly at one another in absolute adoration.

After a while I realized that the language of love, while it has a lot to do with body language and the French kiss, can only take you so far down the path to intimacy. Nope, you have to jump in and learn the language so it becomes a part of you. The intimacy was something else I had to learn.

The language became easier for me. Well, I still make plenty of mistakes but because I was surrounded by people who didn't like to speak English, or couldn't speak English, I was propelled into at least faking it. Believe me, after a short while of only being able to smile at people… I realized I had to make more of an effort. And I did, and it was our first hurdle that we would overcome. But love, falling in love with Philippe and my new circumstances was hardly a hurdle. It was an evolution, a lesson in letting go and in trusting again, but it never felt like an obstacle. In fact, it felt more like a great Harlequin Romance novel, except it was my picture that was on the front of the book.

Chapter 15: In The Dark

You will never be happy if you continue to search for what happiness consists of. You will never live if you are looking for the meaning of life. ~Albert Camus

A journey is best measured in friends, rather than miles.
~ Tim Cahill

No TV.... no TV? What to do?

Being a TV Producer without a TV was really odd, to say the least. Even just being an avid TV viewer who had grown accustomed to the constant background noise meant that I had to make some adjustments; I was minimally profoundly aware of its absence. It often seemed like a black-hole. Frankly, there were nights when Philippe was at work, that I just wanted to bond with the couch, and watch the tube. I missed knowing what was going on in the world too.

The fact that my language skills left much to be desired, it could have helped me learn, it could have been a great tool to utilize. A TV also would have given me insights into the culture and would have assisted me in countless ways I have yet to calculate. Mostly, I think having a TV would have allowed me to be entertained without having to think so hard... something I had to do, while learning the language.

On occasion my friends Gregory and Laurence would invite me to their home to watch a mini-series or a movie. Yes, I got over my beach-boob-moment with Gregory and we became friends; I'm a highly evolved world-traveler now. Anyway, I would jump at the chance to watch TV. It was so funny that watching TV had been elevated to a night out. It was good for me to watch television, it helped me learn the language and become aware of new sayings. Having all of the visual cues was a great aid in my understanding.

I would say that their mini-series where just as schmaltzy as ours, that their commercials were rather sophisticated and I also noted that an ad for yogurt would come up during every commercial break. Probably, the work of the French Food God - no doubt. Other than that, it was just TV. It was great to watch classic U.S. TV shows dubbed in French. Even *Who's the Boss?* in French, is incredibly charming.

The other alternative was to go to the movies. I had heard that there was a cinema on the Island, but where? Finally one night at the restaurant someone came in and dropped off flyers. I asked a friend what that was about and they explained. On the Island there was one cinema that had two theaters inside. Each week they would hand out flyers that listed the various movies that were playing there. I'd say in the course of one week they would have, approximately ten different films. This was a great find! Now I just needed to get up the nerve to go.

As luck would have it, my friend Barbara wanted to take her two amazing kids, Raphael and Nicolas, (Four and six years old) to the movies. These boys have become sort of adopted nephews and I spend a great deal of time with them. Barbara and I became friends for a variety of reasons, one simple truth was that her English was probably better than anybody else on the Island and also she was very artistic and creative, something I completely related to. The fact that she had two adorable young boys who I loved to hang around with- well, that was a major bonus for me.

Raphael is very aware of me and my lack of language skills. He is always very sensitive to that, constantly reminding his brother Nicolas to speak slowly to me. It is kind of embarrassing when a four year old understands that he has a better vocabulary than you do. But Raphael was adorable about it, attentive actually. If truth be told, Raphael has a bit of a crush on me, and I him.

So on this night, the movie was *Bambi*. I figure this should be a reasonably easy movie to understand. First we enter the miniature building which housed the two theaters. The entire building is probably smaller than a standard Pizza Hut in The US. It's small.

Barbara approaches the window and asks for four tickets. I noticed a few bags of candy inside the booth with the gentleman, but I had no idea why he would have them in there with him. Then I start to look for the concession stand so I could treat the boys to some popcorn. Then I figured it must be in another room, as this was a sort of narrow hallway. There was something missing though and I finally realized that it was the smell- what was it? It was the lack of popcorn smell. Where was the popcorn? I asked Barbara where the concession stand was and she didn't understand what I was asking. Despite her command of the English language and my improved French (Vocabulary count 377) there were some words, neither one of us could find. I figured, I'd just let it go, we were bound to bump into it between here and the entrance to the cinema.

Wrong again. We walked straight into this tiny theater that housed about seventy seats and we got settled. There was no concession stand. Perhaps this was another secret finally revealed by the French Food God. I don't know, but I'm not that keen on it, either way.

Raphael sat to my left, Nicolas to my right. I sat in the middle, trying to figure out, how people go to the movies without eating popcorn. First there was a series of commercials (And this was way before we had them in The States), so I watched ad after ad, in shock. Most of it was for chocolate or ice-cream, but it was an endless stream of them, I would say at least twenty minutes had passed before they were over. Then the lights came on a woman magically appeared carrying chocolates and ice-cream cones in a box that was supported by a strap around her neck. You know like the 'cigar-cigarette' case lady you'd find in one of those 1950's movie about Las Vegas? (Yeah, one of those). She walked up and down the aisle and people bought the very same chocolates that were just advertised on the big screen. And people bought ice-cream. Ice-cream cones at the movies. I don't know why but I think there is something wrong with that. Where the hell is the popcorn? Anyway, this roving concession stand scene went on for a good ten minutes or so and I just watched the entire process, in awe.

Finally the lights dimmed and everyone relaxed. As soon as the movie started, I heard this little voice in my left ear. It was Raphael, who was doing his very best to explain everything that was happening on the big screen. He was so sweet and it was so funny. He basically repeated each word, nice and slow, with a deliberate, clear delivery. He gave an explanation for each and every scene and I managed to keep a straight face. Finally, Raphael sniffled a bit and managed to eek-out, "La mère de Bambi est mort." The death of Bambi's mother is obviously one of the most famously sad moments in American film history, upsetting to all who witness it. The fact that Raphael wanted to help to cushion the blow and guide me through this traumatic, melancholy moment, bonded us forever.

I loved every second of *Bambi*, I got to see it through Raphael's eyes and it was great. And I also fell even more in love with Raphael as he showed me just how much he cared for me and wanted to protect and serve me, if even just to translate *Bambi*.

I did go to the theater a lot after that. I remember on the next trip to the cinema, I went by myself. I was prepared for no-popcorn. The movie was *A River Runs Through It*, Brad Pitt speaking French... do you think I really cared that I didn't understand what they were saying? After that, I happily waited for the weekly-movie flyer to be distributed. It would help me determine my schedule for the entire week. I always looked so forward to reading the flyer; it was like being a kid on Christmas morning, unwrapping a precious gift, I could hardly wait just to see what they deemed cinema-worthy.

That tiny island theater meant I could go and see endless movies dubbed in French; it was a life-saver. For me it offered a great night out. It gave me a break from having to really think, a break from participating in conversations where my brain had to be on, full tilt-working. I could just sit back, absorb, relax and learn. I also got a night off from worrying about potentially embarrassing myself. There was magic in that theater.

It was there, in the dark, that I learned a lot about the French language and also about how much Raphael cared for me. And it was there that I learned how to go to the movies without popcorn, talk about evolved.

Chapter 16: La Fête de la Musique

Talking about music is like dancing about architecture.
~Steve Martin

Let us be grateful to people who make us happy; they are the charming gardeners who make our souls blossom. ~Marcel Proust

Being the only American within many, many miles has one or two advantages. I felt like I was a celebrity of sorts which is odd coming from Manhattan where being anonymous is so much a part of the gig there. Philippe used to come home from work, in the early days and ask me how my day at the beach, grocery store etc. was. Was he psychic or a stalker? He'd know so many details about what I wore etc., it was a tad creepy until he told me his source.

Check this out, the farmer-gentleman who used to stand on the corner in Le Deux or hang out at the weird-ass grocery/bar/café would discuss what "The American" was up to. Since we lived in a village of fifty, I was big news on the farmer-gentleman's report. Word would travel through the Island, as apparently they had little else to discuss. It was really odd and kind of funny and just a wee bit unnerving. But everyone knew that an American lived on the Island. For a lot of the farmers and fisherman, they had only seen an American on TV or in the movies before. So to have a real-live American to look at was really something. Odd as that seems it was exciting for them and awkward and a bit much for me to get used to. Regardless of how I felt about it, there was no way I was flying below anyone's radar here.

And being the expert on English also made me sort of a roving librarian... if you will. The French would ask me about all sorts of stuff; trivia questions, historical facts, grammar, politics, geography and reference questions, really- nothing was off-limits. They would ask about movies, and movie stars, fashion and New York itself, they'd ask about the American dream and anything else they could come up with. But my favorite query, from friends and strangers alike was 'What are they saying in this song?'

As you know- music is worldly, it's cross-cultural and it defies borders; but often times, it doesn't translate- in fact, it can be really difficult to understand.

The fact is that, American music is very popular in France, even on l'île d'Oléron, so they would hear music ranging from hip hop to old Beatles songs, and sort of know the words, or think they knew the lyrics, but not really. It didn't stop them from enjoying it though. If they knew the lyrics, they didn't necessarily know the meaning. So they'd come to me, their one-stop-shopping roving reference American library-lady and ask; I loved it. Try to imagine with my broken French translating:

> I said a hip hop the hippie the hippie to the hip hip hop, a you don't stop the rock it to the bang bang boogie say up jumped the boogie to the rhythm of the boogie, the beat now what you hear is not a test—I'm rapping to the beat and me, the groove, and my friends are

gonna try to move your feet see I am Wonder Mike and I like to say hello to the black, to the white, the red, and the brown, the purple and yellow but first I gotta bang bang the boogie to the boogie say up jump the boogie to the bang bang boogie let's rock, you don't stop (etc. etc.)

I can't even translate that to English. SO it was kind of a hilarious task but one I adored. It was also comical to hear how they interpreted the songs, or messed up the lyrics, but also it was seriously-cute. It was one of those cultural things that the misunderstanding made it endearing. And their love of American music was something we could share.

I went to a party one night without Philippe, because he was working (again) and basically he said- if I was invited to a party then I had to go. He said he'd meet me there later- but I'd have to walk through the door and get through the first few hours, solo. I knew nothing about protocol but I basically tried to get out of going. I tried to get-away with getting there late... and I was told that this would be considered as a huge insult. Anyway, I went. I bought a huge bouquet of flowers and held my breath when I walked through the door. My friends Gregory and Laurence were hosting and they made me feel welcome despite the fact that I could hardly hold any sort of real conversation. Let's face it; it was easier to watch TV with them, then to tackle a big crowd of people without Philippe by my side. They had a cute little apartment on the second floor above a small shop right off of the main square in St. Piérre, perfect. I climbed the stairs, took a gulp of air and pushed my anxiety down while I pushed myself through the door.

Steph, Gregory's brother, promptly started plying me with drinks. (Love that guy) Gregory, who was pretty much one of the few people good as speaking English; (Second only to Barbara) would often take it upon himself to sit near me and wade through the conversation. So between Gregory watching over my shoulder to assist with translations and Steph there to assist with my cocktail consumption, I was being taken care of.

That night someone was there playing guitar and some folks were singing along. This has always been something I love,

love, love to do. And when they starting botching every song from *Bridge Over Troubled Water* to *Let It Be*, I was called in to clarify the lyrics. Not only did this give me great pleasure it gave me something to do with myself at this party where I was feeling awkward and shy. It seemed that I would be unable to remain a wall-flower with my #1 U.S. status.

And so it began and as long as I was there to translate lyrics I began singing them along with Goutier the guitarist. Everyone was thrilled, for them it was tapping into a treasure chest filled with long lost lyrics and for me? I was having a blast singing along. They all thought I should join Goutier during the course of the summer to sing curbside for the tourists. You know the drill, with a little jar out on the road. But I am way to uncomfortable with singing publicly to do that, but this, this was very cool. By the time Philippe showed up I was jamming and indeed, the life of the party. He laughed and I think he felt relieved for me because he understood how nervous I was to go it alone. As a side bar: because I am so outgoing it is impossible for people to see me as shy or having shy moments, but believe me, I can and I do. And this had been one of them, until we started singing the top forty.

The very next day, as luck would have it, was La Fête de la Musique. This fantastic French holiday happens every June 21. In every town, and every village or city street you'll hear music, it is a total celebration of just that; music, in every form. You'll hear big bands, and blues and random people will stroll the narrow cobbled streets playing tubas and bagpipes and flutes. Likewise major concerts can happen in some of the bigger cities or even in the small village squares.

What a fantastic holiday, this is something everyone should celebrate. I know people love to pick on the French for a variety of reasons, but this? How could you not give the French credit for La Fête de la Musique? This outstanding holiday should put them on the map as the smartest people on the planet. Who can argue with the merriment of music? Young, old, smart, stupid, black, white, and any religious background or a lack-there-of, and political orientation, anyone, everyone can identify and appreciate this holiday. Fantastic.

This would be my first ever, so seeing choruses of young people or guitarists ramble down the street singing was pure magic. Of course Philippe was working, but his core group of like fourteen friends, were going to go to the restaurant that night to celebrate. The restaurant, Le Forum as mentioned, was located just on the town square of St. Piérre, the main village of the Island. It had a café that faced a huge parking lot that doubled as the town square and the farmer's market on Tuesdays. The inside of the restaurant was brightly lit, so the outside was much cozier. The late summer sunset and fantastic Oléron light provided an incredible backdrop. I'd watch the conversation around the table and then my eye would drift towards the purple hue as it would take over the sky well past 10:30pm just after sunset.

Tonight in the gazebo/band-shell that was in the center of the square, it was music city. So as we sat drinking wine (With a hint of cassis) and eating our lovely meal; we heard all sorts of different music being played. School bands, jazz music, the air was filled with a merry melody and we were getting merrier on the wine.

What a riot, this is one cool place to be, and I was having the best time. It took three hours to finish our meal and Philippe was done with work. I was happy to have him join us as we all walked over to the gazebo to enjoy the music. About 250 people were dancing and laughing and some of the other restaurant cafés were still filled with people laughing and eating.

A relatively good blues band started to play and everyone was having fun. The square was filled with a vibrant sound and the gazebo was lit with multi-color stage lights. The lead singer engaged the crowd so well. I remember he said something in French to the crowd. I didn't technically understand, but it did register at some core-level of my being. In my mind I heard, 'Would anyone like to join us up here and sing?' Instinctively I knew enough to back away and remove myself from the crowd and as I took one step I saw Gregory, Steph and Lauren (Another surfer) coming to grab me to pull me toward the stage. They literally dragged me and forced me on stage. This was by far, the very last thing I wanted to do.

I was literally hauled up on stage with my heels digging into the town-square's asphalt. I was pulled up onto the stage by the bandleader and I looked at him as if I was a dear, caught in the headlights. Just so you know, I was wearing a fabulous outfit, very New York all the way, so retro, I can hardly tell you; cut-off jean shorts with dark black tights underneath, and black boots that stopped at the ankles, very Madonna-ish. I didn't make up the style, I just followed it.

I sported a fabulous Betsey Johnson sassy shirt with Philippe's leather biker jacket to finish it off. I looked like a rock-star. I did not look anything like anyone else on the Island. In fact, Philippe had heard what I was wearing before I got to the restaurant that night, because the farmers were in quite-the-buzz about it.

Anyway, time began to move very slowly and I think the lead singer said something like, sing any song, and we'll follow you. Now out of the 274- million plus songs or so that I have stored in my roving librarian-brain, wouldn't you know not one of them would come up to the surface. I smiled, I told the guy I didn't really speak French and he smiled, I was clearly without any of my French vocabulary at the moment. The crowd, which held at least twenty people that I sort of knew, (At least well-enough to kiss hello) started chanting "Allez Judith!" until all 250 people were yelling.

They were playing blues and I started barely squeaking out *Stormy Monday*. I heard my voice softly in the microphone and then playing back in the speakers; the sound seemed to startle me. I think I sort of got some of the lyrics right. It's OK though, no-one knows the difference anyway. Then the crowd chanted "Mustang Sally" which apparently was a big hit from the party just the night before. On this one, I tried my best to belt it out as I got more comfortable on the stage. "Guess you gotta slow that mustang down," and with one last "ride Sally ride" which I was now singing in harmony with the lead singer, I smiled and walked off stage. I think my heart started to beat again. The crowd went crazy, and I, in my fabulous New York City-centric outfit, managed not to trip on my way down the stairs.

Just a short time in France and I have now officially performed –this is an alternate universe. Paule and Firmin actually heard all about it too. When I ran into Philippe's parents the next day on the beach, they couldn't wait to ask me about it. This was big news for the Island and a big departure for me.

For weeks after that every time I went into our regular hangout, my friend Barbara's husband's club 'Le Transat' which always had live music, I would have this palpable fear of being dragged onto the stage. They would taunt me and tease me, so I would walk out to the parking lot, and hangout there.

There was always a good size crowd who had spilled outside for some air or to smoke. They smoked everywhere so they really spoiled the air both inside and out of La Transat; but outside you could at least grab a little oxygen simultaneously. I really didn't want to sing in public again, and after a while I made my new French friends promise me that they wouldn't force me. Regardless of my fear, for that one night I was a fucking rock star.

Friday in France

Chapter 17: American Independence

Freedom is nothing else but a chance to be better. ~ *Albert Camus*

Curious things, habits, people themselves never knew they had them.
~ *Agatha Christie*

As July 4th came into view I realized that I wouldn't be celebrating American Independence Day. Although, one could certainly argue that I had become independent of America in my own recent history (sort-of.) It was weird to think that there would be no fireworks, no BBQs and no cans of Budweiser to be had. The holiday itself, has no real meaning to me other than it marks the summer season and always was a good time. I didn't even realize that I would miss it until it became obvious that I wouldn't be celebrating. No biggie, Bastille Day, the nationally celebrated French holiday would come a few weeks later, as would the fireworks etc. OK so July 14th would offer fireworks, but what about that BBQ?

I decided to take advantage of the fact that July 4th was coming and invite a few friends over to our garden and to make a little BBQ anyway. I'd use it as an excuse to have people over and entertain for the first time and I decided to make it an-all American-fest. I'd do that for a few reasons. 1) No way could I attempt French cooking and out-cook the French and 2) Maybe it'd be fun to share an American tradition. Most importantly I wanted to thank people for being so gracious and welcoming me into their circle.

I decided to move forward and make a shopping list- that meant I'd have to figure out what to serve. I went with chicken kabobs (as to up-grade it a bit) and of course some traditional hotdog and hamburgers. What would the 4th be like without corn-on-the cob? I didn't know and wasn't willing to find out. That being said, I decided to introduce some islanders to s'mores as well. Why not? Super, messy, super-sticky and super-American and probably due to the mess of it all- made is super anti-French.

Shopping for these items would be my first task. I decided to aim to the farmer's market because I felt like I could get the bulk of what I needed and then that would leave me with just a few items to deal with at the grocery store, which was not my favorite of all places to go to. I still had a lot of learning to do when it came to the French grocery store. The farmer's market offered plenty of goodies, and I enjoyed shopping there. I did have to veto the hotdogs and go with chorizo because that was the closest thing I could find... but that's fine. It took me some time to find corn-on-the-cob, but once I finally found it at a road-side stand, I completed my list.

Philippe, as per usual at this point, would be at work. As the season was starting to approach, he would be there more and more. He went to work twice a day, from 10am until 2 or 3pm. Then back at 6pm until anywhere from ten to midnight, depending on how busy things were.

This meant that I had to solidify relationships and create a social-network for myself, he appreciated my efforts. Truth be told- I did it for me, I need to be social. Having this BBQ was part of that and also I just wanted a little 4th of July for myself.

Gregory and his girlfriend Laurence and Steph were invited. I also invited our surfer friend Lauren, and the twin girls Stephanie and Gaelle, who were there from Paris. That would be enough for a first time effort. I worked most of the day to make sure everything was perfect. Getting the grill fired up would be the one-chore I would ask one of my more-manly guests to tackle. Everything else was ready to go so I could enjoy my guests. I bought plenty of beer and wine (No Budweiser though) and I figured the rest would just flow.

It doesn't get dark out this time of year on the Island until almost 11pm, which is fabulous. It also means it will be hot and sunny in our garden. Beer was a great idea.

I explained to them that it was the 4th of July, this was an attempt to bring a little of my homeland to them and so they needed to forgive the menu a bit. In fact, I wanted them to go with it and to embrace their inner-American. Everyone was cool with that, but I noticed the corn-on-the-cob went untouched. Now to me, grilled corn -on-the-cob is sweet and special and I did have to travel across the Island to find it. Finally Gregory clued me in. Corn-on-the-cob happens to be difficult to find and wildly unappetizing to my guests because, here- it is only fed to the hogs. Come to think of it- the farmer gave me an odd look when I bought it at the road-side stand. I had already grown accustomed to farmers (and others) looking at me like I was weird. Besides, I thought it was very country-ish. My friends found it a bit bizarre that Americans would consider eating pig-slop.

OK, well moving on then... to the s'mores. Knowing how neat and proper the French are, I admit that I was relying on their sense of adventure and curiosity about Americans to even give it a try. That and the fact that I had no alternate dessert to offer were part of my plan. Plus they always must end their meal with some kind of dessert, just ask the French Food God. The French use a fork and knife in a very proper way to consume 99% of what they eat. This means learning how to balance peas on the back of a fork. Even two year old children hold their silverware in a formal manner that 98% of the American population, know nothing about. So holding a sticky s'more with your hands was a pretty wild and crazy concept.

The cooked marshmallows forced the chocolate to melt between the pseudo graham-crackers, (I couldn't find the exact real deal) but the sloppiness and the melted droppings did their trick. I think the beer did too, because everyone raved. They loved it. You see the French really love to know about Americans and how we live etc. So the positioning of the s'mores and the event of the 4th really helped to sell it. I was kind-of an American public relations officer on my way to changing the French perception... one s'more at a time. Top political spin-doctors could learn a few tricks from me. I gave the left over corn to our farmer-neighbors to feed the little pigs they had. They took it and smiled, and graciously accepted my offering. I am sure they wondered why it was grilled.

Chapter 18: Back to the Boob Thing

Humor is reason gone mad. ~Groucho Marx

Twenty years from now you will be more disappointed by the things that you didn't do than by the ones you did do. So throw off the bowlines. Sail away from the safe harbor. Catch the trade winds in your sails. Explore. Dream. Discover. ~ Mark Twain

Can we go back to the boob thing for a moment? Please, as if you could stop me. Of course we can, how can I not? By now I'm an old pro at baring my naked breasts; oh I still have that occasional embarrassing moment. Maybe even ridiculously long drawn out moments that only fifteen years of therapy with a New York Upper West Side shrink will cure, but still I've made incredible progress. All in all I've come to get used to it, I want my breasts to be tan, evenly brown and fabulous. For that matter, I'd also like them to be perky- but these *bad-boys* came in as low riders, so there is really no non-surgical hope for that. Even the powerful sun can't shrink them up a few inches, no matter how much I might burn them.

I've decided to stick with my plan, be patient and use the sun block so I won't burn my nipples off, all-n-all a fairly levelheaded idea. I just pray that they'll catch up to my full body tan, soon! By soon, I mean... yesterday.

Nope, with my luck I develop a rash, yes, a rash on my chest. Let me clarify what I mean by rash; some sort of eruption on my skin. Some over-speckled red-raised dots that have been splashed all over my chest; a dreaded skin condition of sorts highlighted by spots, blotches, red-in-nature... all over my frickin' body. I can't believe my eyes, most likely from A) oily sun block, B) over exposure to the sun C) some deep hidden psychosomatic reaction stemming from a boob-less bathing childhood D)possibly all of the above.

Either way, I've got a rash, and when I say, I've got it, trust me I've got it. I have tried hydrocortisone cream, zit cream (?) a drying agent, but no, this fricking rash is a stubborn red dot parade and it is ready to stay for the long haul. It mocks me. You may think I jest, but I do not, my rash, mocks me, as if to say, "Your boobs are American, now get them back inside your bathing suit before we tell your Mother!"

Maybe it is all part of some grand cosmic joke... a test of my comfort level, maybe the French Food God is behind all of this. This week, come to think of it, hasn't been a good week for my body, at all; this is a gross understatement at that. One accident has followed the next. I burned my leg on the BMW's metal something or other, with my motorcycle dismount on Monday; this, after a two-hour butt-numbing ride through the countryside. The fact that I couldn't feel my thighs when I was getting off of the damned thing, probably had something to do with it. I got my period ragging that night, and then jammed my foot into a rock on the beach and broke my toe in the process. I was probably worried about showing my rash-covered chest in public. I have since taped up my little toe and I did my best, but it still looks clunky in sandals. I suppose, that is the least of it. I'm all too aware that it is just Wednesday afternoon, and I have a long way to go to finish out the week.

By Thursday night the boob-rash was full blown, by full blown I mean, you've got to be kidding me. And then, wouldn't you know it, the mini-van ran out of gas. Luckily I was really close to the gas station and it was still open. But by early Friday, after my solo mini-van-gas-station-push, I was feeling a bit tapped out. Sure, I could proudly announce that I was no longer a virgin mini-van-gas-station-pusher, but what good did that do me? And surprise, surprise, I must have pulled something in my back while manually moving the mini-van, bravo.

Friday night rolls around; there I am with my burnt leg, broken toe, powerful period, big-boob-rash and pulled muscle in my back... and this is when I finally get my chance to jump–start the mini-van, again. Seriously, are the planets lined up against me or what? All I know is all of this has me feeling the need for comfort food.

If this is the work of that damned French Food God, then I suppose I need to start consuming goose pâté, and bobbing bread in my bowl-of-hot chocolate or something. Lord, give me a break, what could an egg cooked on top of a pizza loaded with cream have to do with my current state? Am I to take from this –that I'm not going with the French flow of things?

I believe I have made a sincere attempt to embrace and even tackle (In some cases) French culture. I've agreed (Thus far) to drive off the road if another baby car approaches. I've agreed that tanned boobs are a good thing. I've even come to adore a few new apéritífs, like the martini rouge for example. Add to that, I've agreed to go on several back-fender, missing-a-seat, butt-numbing rides on Philippe's BMW. I feel like I am committed to the French way!

Perhaps I should just BE committed, instead. You do the math, but at this point, I feel like I've done my part and that I should get some break from this downward spiraling motion that I feel as of late. I sit and reflect on the week and the vortex I seem to be based-in and I can't help wonder, what is going on?

Dear FFG, (French Food God)

As you know dieting has been my goal, and I have been really good. I am not sure what is up though, as I have been having a rough week. I will admit a while ago that I did try to serve pig-food to dinner guests. In my defense though, this was an innocent mistake and actually it was an attempt to share one of my favorite summer 4th of July treats. My heart was clearly in the right place.

Anyway, forgive me but I just want to point out a few things that might convince you to give me a break. What you might not be taking note of, and I think you should give me some credit for, is my embracing the French way. I have tried many new things. I have. I've pushed my gas-less mini-van into the station by myself. While this isn't directly related to food, I was on my way to the grocery store at the time and I did have to get there before they closed for the afternoon siesta. I bought bread and promptly placed it in my armpit, while it was hot mind you. And when I broke my toe the other day, I swore in French!

OK so, I may need to repent on some of my sins though. One in particular may not have thrilled you. It is true that I had a taste of milk-chocolate, (Bypassing dark chocolate) I did however allow myself to savor every bite, and to keep the record straight, I was having my frickin' period, so give me a break. Everyone should be allowed period-chocolate.

Throughout this past accident-filled week it dawned on me that perhaps something is wrong. Perhaps all these accidents indicate that the universe, the cosmos at large, is trying to let me know that I am doing something wrong. I do feel as though my efforts to exercise should be rewarded with a size two dress-size by next Thursday. Don't get me wrong, I am aware that exercise is not actually part of The Ten Commandments and that French women do not part-take... but I have been working my tushie off (literally) none-the-less. I would also like to request that my boobs magically become rash free, if not today, certainly by tomorrow. I am down seven lbs. and that's quite good –right? I wonder, if I make you a crêpe as a sacrifice of sorts, will you give me some kind of extra credit? Please let me know if any of this moves you.

With hunger and thirst to please you, sincerely,

The rash-covered, mini-van pushing, irritated American

I take one look up towards the sky making a formal prayer like pose and then I look down at my rash covered boobs and hope that the crêpe sacrifice will do the trick. I decide not to go out tonight, a rare occasion indeed. I just lock myself in the baby-house, without any sharp objects and do nothing else to tempt the gods. Especially the FFG, lord knows I don't want to mangle myself any further.

Friday in France

Chapter 19: Grocery Shopping

France has found a unique way of controlling its unwanted critter population. They have done this by giving unwanted animals like snails, pigeons, and frogs fancy names, thus transforming common backyard pests into expensive delicacies. These are then served to gullible tourists, who will eat anything they can't pronounce.
~Chris Harris

Traveling is almost like talking with men of other centuries.
~Rene Descartes

You think it is a challenge to go to the grocery store in The U.S.? Ha! The worst thing is you might not be able to get a primo parking space or the wheel on your cart may not cooperate as you'd like. In New York City, you won't even bother to buy that much because you have to carry it home, so in that case, maybe your back will hurt after carrying your milk eight blocks... big deal.

On the Island, my first few trips to the grocery store where quite interesting. First, I didn't even attempt to get a cart because from a distance I could see that it costs ten French Francs. That's two dollars U.S., hell; I'll carry my own crap. Add to that, there is some special place you have to get and return your cart from and it appears that all the carts are chained up in a tangled mess. It looks really complicated and believe me, it is beyond my comprehension at this point. I definitely don't want to ask anyone about it, or draw any attention to myself, so I avoid it all together. I can only picture myself struggling with these chains to set my cart free - so I skip it. I buy only a few items and struggle to the register, I figure someday down the road, I'll be brave and attempt to get my cart- but I'll stick to the basics for now. Anyway, we only have a half refrigerator at home, that houses little, and I eat out 90% of the time so that combined with my extreme diet-plan has kept me from a really big grocery shopping mission, until now.

Besides, there are so many other things I need to focus on here; I have to pace my learning curve. I need to figure out how much humiliation a gal can take.

Then after a few a few months of being on various mini fact finding-missions, I feel like I am ready to take on 'the big shop,' a bigger plunge than normal. I need to start with the basics and review some of what I know: the store opens at 7am or 8am depending on the owner. They all seem to close at noon and re-open at 3pm and close again at 7pm. There is no 7/11 to stop in if you forget something, which I will, every time. I haven't noticed any postings on the store hours and nothing to notify me that the store is open and closed more frequently than makes sense, it is just commonly understood, I think.

For me, if I manage to arrive at the grocery store when it is open I feel like I've won the damned lotto. So groovy, if I can just manage to get there when it's open, that'll be a good start. I have the uncanny and consistent knack of arriving at 12:10pm Remember I come from the city that never sleeps... you can grocery shop in New York at 5am. Add to that, Philippe and I often stay out or up until 4am or so, jumping out of bed early in the morning, isn't top on my priority list.

Anyway, let's assume on this one day, I finally manage to get there around 11am conceivably leaving me enough time to do a real-grocery shop. Note to self: For those who were brave enough to rescue a cart from the chain link zone they do not appear to struggle with just one wheel, but all four, the entire contraption has to be pushed along on a forty-five degree angle. The good news is, here you get your aerobic exercise in at the same time as you muscle your cart down the aisle. So if you get to the store during the hours of operation and you manage to maneuver your cart out of the chain-chaos area and down the aisles, I'd say you're a super star. But for today, maybe I'll just pass on the cart again. I know... I'm a big-baby.

Now, let's approach the fruit and vegetable section. Here people weigh their own fruit etc. Of course not in pounds because they use the metric system, and I have no idea how that scale works, but I'll hang back and watch a few folks go through it and see if I can gain some insight from observing their hands-on experience. Since I am extremely serious about my dieting veggies are big on my list today. OH yeah, I notice that the scale is set up with corresponding pictures... made for those who speak any language and so even those who cannot form sentences can operate this! Yeah-that's me!

Thank goodness I do not need to know that a potato is called a pommes-de-terre etc., because we would really be limited to approximately three vegetables at our house. And even if I know by now what it is called, I sure don't know how to spell it because I've learned to speak by listening, not attending a school and certainly not from reading. So picture-coded shopping is perfect for me! Looks like I just find the picture and go. Find a picture and go... kind of a preschool version of food shopping, I like it!

Shit, I've already got more than I can carry and as I begin to fumble the produce. I decide I really need to just head back towards the poor chained up carts. They look so sad, they do. I remind myself that the farmers will have a field day with the American-report if I get caught with melons rolling down the aisle and so I cautiously move closer to the carts.

I mean how difficult can this be? I don't really want to know the answer to that. I put my veggies down and then I put the ten French Franc coin into the slot. It irks me that this is costing me $2. It is the principle of the matter. I some-how manage to detangle the metal shackles, clearly all that working-out is paying off. I am Wonder Woman… I can hear the theme song in my head. I place my veggies into the insanely difficult to control cart and bravely head toward the bakery. Luckily it is only a few feet away as my cart is seriously challenged.

At the bakery … the odor leaves you weak in the knees, not to mention the stomach. I believe I was actually hypnotized by the aroma. What I don't get is why people are paying for their baked-goods here and not at the front register. Crap, was I supposed to pay for the veggies somewhere back in vegetable land? How would I know and who is to say and who can I ask? No one, I feel so stupid. I decide to push on then; upward and onward through the grocery aisles. I can go to the local patisserie later this afternoon and I'm already used to that, they already know me there… just point and pay… much easier.

OK here is an aisle I can hang around for a while; we got wine, beer, apéritifs, all for the taking. But I am lost with all the selections. I can't really read packages yet, so I continue; I push my crap cart at a seventy-five degree angle and watch what other people buy. I grab a few bottles of wine that a young woman buys… she looks normal, and I have no other way of judging things currently so off I go.

Moving on: milk and eggs, ah milk and eggs, how complicated can that be? Well interestingly enough either are not refrigerated. I look around, no one seems alarmed. I am however put-off by this. I'll grab some now and will ask questions later when Philippe gets home. Maybe I should get a note pad to track my questions. What aisle would I find a note pad on? Forget it.

I come across the yogurt aisle. Holy Moly! I think I hear angels playing the harp in the background. This aisle must be worshipping grounds for those who idolize the French Food God. It is the biggest aisle in the history of yogurt. Oh for the love of yogurt. This explains the non-stop TV commercials. Good, OK, this should be easy to find something I like, let me find a fat free yogurt and move on. Fat-Free MY NON-FAT-FREE-Ass. After ten minutes of serious dedication to the cause I realize, I'm not going to find fat-free yogurt unless I hop a plane back to The U.S. OK so a bit of a paradox in paradise, impressive ode to yogurt and yet, they are lacking in the low-fat, no-fat choice category. How can you have a complete aisle dedicated to yogurt and not one fat-free fricking yogurt? Not a comprehensive yogurt collection if you ask me. Boy, do the French love their yogurt though. My eyes are drawn to the Petíte Dannon thing... it is the size of half of a shot glass. It must be super-powered yogurt that fills you up before you open it. I don't know, but I'm not buying that one either. I'm kinda pissed at the lack of fat-free yogurt... I'm on a yogurt strike. (Take that FFG!)

The snack aisle- hmm.... did I miss that? OH no, here it is... approx. three tiny shelves with little bags of chips on it. Weird chips too, but I am amazed by the lack of choice or stock. I hope there isn't a sign that says limit, *one bag per customer.* The chip section is about the same size section where we would keep our Fabric Softener. No more, no less, and this is for the entire neighborhood? WOW, FFG, you have just given away one of the big French food secrets to skinny success. I bow my head, roll my eyes and sigh in disbelief.

I can't believe this damned cart cost me two bucks and I can't get it to go even remotely straight and now, there is a chip shortage too. I don't know if I can bare it. To add insult to injury they have peanut butter Cheetos or something close to that and I do not think this is a translation issue for me... I'm looking at a picture on the package... and I'm moving on. When we have people over later in the week, I'll go with olives... I like that better anyway.

Well, I think I do not have the heart to really continue too much longer. I'll just grab some cheese (Of which there are only 2,104,717 choices) and about seven people who are standing there opening packages and smelling them. I stop cold in my tracks, maybe the cheese purchase is more complicated then I first imagined. Stunned, I stare as people open the container and put their nose right up to it, and smell. I'm talking less than a quarter inch from the actual cheese itself, yup, they put their nose in and inhale. They don't make a secret of it either, this isn't some undercover mission. It isn't the equivalent of us stealing M&Ms from the bulk candy area and hoping no one notices. Nope, it is a complete public display of cheese smelling. Apparently a tradition of sorts, I find this to be a dreadful practice. Even if I did want to smell the cheese, and frankly, I don't, what would I be smelling for? Anyway, I know that I really don't want to have to deal with any of the farmer's wives especially while they are smelling cheese and I don't want to sniff it either. I want to go home. I reach in the back, the very back of the cheese section and hope the package I select hasn't been 'pre-smelled' by anyone. The thought sends shivers up my spine.

OK I'm going to make my way to the check-out counter. I should mention that there are some universal things about grocery shopping. For example when you see a sign that says *eight items only*, you really don't need to be able to read the language to understand. All you need to do is look at the long line of people with eight items, and the one or two idiots with baskets filled with at least seventeen items in there to know. You can read it on the faces of those who are following the rules. You can see the dislike for the rule breakers, as they stare in their direction. The helpless cashier is too smart, lazy or scared to say anything and so it goes. That is universal.

Here in France when people pay with credit cards they give a code not a signature (Actually a damned smart idea.) And the French seem to pay for everything with their credit cards, even or especially their groceries. So I can't tell which line says cash only or which line says credit cards only, and I just avoid the line that appears to be the limit on the number of items. No clue, and this cart has actually twisted itself to a full 80-degree angle now (Not in a favorable direction) and somehow I have to get it on track to squeeze through checkout.

For a moment I reflect on how distressing this all is. I have a college degree, a very successful career as a manager at NBC and I am feeling beyond overwhelmed trying to accomplish my first real big grocery store trip. The part that makes me a tad-bit ashamed is that I have actually been warming up for this over the past several mini-visits.

Let's face it, I like to look cool, or minimally just blend-in, who doesn't? And the fact that I can't tell what's in this tiny yogurt or why people are smelling cheese, or how to get my cart to go reasonably straight makes me look anything but, cool. I feel super-lame right now. I want to go home and smell my cheese in private and see if I can crack the code.

Clueless I stand, trying to get my shoulders back in position, to at least look confident. I help by removing my groceries from the cart. I wait for her or someone to begin bagging the items…. but it isn't happening. She tosses a few bags my way, and I surmise that, I to do the packing.

She finishes checking me out I pay; this is always awkward because I don't have a code for my credit card, which means everyone gets confused, and I have to explain myself and then they KNOW I am American, the only American. The American, the very same American of which they have endless stories about and then they stare… my groceries are still all over the place and she begins with the next person. Ok… I get it, really-really, no help from anyone; my groceries start to get pushed aside I just slam them into my cart.

I go as fast as I can, throwing things into bags to make a graceful exit. I see that some people grab empty boxes found at the front of the store to really organize their haul, but I feel way too much time pressure to be organized now. I finish packing and when I complete the mission I am relieved and push this crap cart out of the store, (Now at an eighty-five degree angle and in desperate need of WD40) toward the parking lot. Not as graceful as I'd like. And it gets harder to push these mad-carts on the asphalt, so I sideways shuffle myself along. Now I come close to where I first got the cart, the chain-link nightmare area, but I am kind of far from my car. It's decision-making time.

I opt to return the cart. It really isn't helping at this point anyway. I try to organize my eight bags and stuff the random items from my cart, into my bags and begin to try to figure out the chain puzzle. I get my cart back in place and bam- as I slip the metal clip into my cart…wouldn't you know it- the ten Franc coin comes back out. It's simply a deposit!! HEY I learned something! Alright! Not a bad concept either, because I note that the parking lot is cart free, everyone wants their money back. I feel like a total idiot for the times I came here before and struggled juggling my items in my hands because I didn't want to pay. Ah well, live it and learn it. C'est la vie!

Now, I lean over to grab the eight bags of poorly packed items; no-one to blame but myself. I struggle to make my way to the car. Between me and the car I notice a pack of gypsy children. Oh no, not the dreaded gypsy children, the *60-Minutes Report* flashes before my eyes. Apparently they like to distract you and pick your pocket; Morley Safer's voice reaches out to warn me. Then, I begin to swing my heavy bags and pull an old NY subway trick. Act like a crazy person, do a crazy walk or make an odd face, or start talking to yourself, or all the above and you will find that magically people will give you space.

And so I, with my eight bags of poorly packed groceries start doing a crazy walk, and wonders of wonders I manage to get to my van. The gypsy children run away because they believe me to be insane. I make it to the van.

Now, I throw the groceries into the back of the mini-van next to one of Philippe's long-boards. I feel like I climbed Mount Everest. Relief washes over me, I have accomplished so much and really so little, all at the same time. I can only imagine what the farmer gentlemen will have to say about me tonight. I take solace in the fact that I can cheese-smell in the privacy of our baby-home, as soon as I get there.

Friday in France

Chapter 20: Toy Soldiers

A journey is like marriage. The certain way to be wrong is to think you control it. ~ John Steinbeck

An adventure is only an inconvenience rightly considered. An inconvenience is only an adventure wrongly considered. ~ G. K. Chesterton

Finally, the last of the papers for the Renault have arrived and I am free to move about the Island in my new, very old, car. Thank you Chef. Philippe makes sure (Several times) that I have everything I need including a complete explanation re: each of the papers and he reminds me to keep them in my possession at all times. He has explained each detail repeatedly to me and I have yet to focus on a word he has said and therefore I have yet to comprehend. He shows me where the jack and spare tire are and now, I am free. I don't have to drive the big-little-mini-van anymore and for that I am extremely grateful. The rest, matters very little to me.

The next night, I drive down the Route National and Philippe is ahead on his BMW. We are making our way to La Transat for a nightcap. I'm solo, and therefore confident and happy that there is no one to yell at me (And I am only skipping 1st gear on occasion I might add). I think I see someone flash their bright lights at me. But, I can't tell, I really don't know- do Frenchies flash? (Lights, that is) In France most headlights are yellow, why- I do not know, who is to say, and maybe it has to do with their love of mustard or something. Anyway, when you run into a set of white headlights they suddenly seem wildly- bright for starters so I can't tell if they are flashing me or not. Night time on the Island roads is very dark. Most streets don't have any street lights so a passing car is something I easily take notice of. So if they are flashing me, what does that mean? In The States I'd slow down thinking radar was up ahead, but I don't even know if they have radar here... or whatever.

I decide to drive with caution either way; after all it has been less than twenty-four hours that I have obtained the proper insurance and paper work. I look maybe fifty feet in front of me and there is a bright large flashlight- a circle of light, a circumference of 25" or so, in the middle of the road. I think construction ahead or maybe an accident; I see a guy dressed in what appears to be a tin helmet with a bright orange vest pointing me into an empty gas station.

Whoa, I'm from the city man; I don't just pull off into parking lots at night because some guy has a big light. But it seems rather official and I seem to be without a choice, so I do. I realize as I pull in that that I am definitely not being offered a choice. I try to avoid car-jacking thoughts as I turn in. Now I see two men wearing tin bucket helmets with chin straps who seem to be asking, no... demanding that I unroll the window. I think, they must be official because their uniforms are so damned ridiculous there is no way they aren't.

By the way, when I say tin-bucket helmets with chin straps, I mean tin-bucket helmets with chin straps; imagine an economy size can of string beans stripped of its label. Picture puncturing either side with a hole and adding a string for a strap... and you are basically getting the picture. I think to myself, is David Lynch shooting a movie in France? Has Candid Camera begun a new series here on the Island?

First I want to panic, but the toy-soldiers and their seriousness force me to hold my laugh, the very laughter that begins deep in my belly that I know I should not and cannot release. Before I can really allow myself to start cracking up – they start yelling in French. It's hard to take people seriously on the job when they have such bad fashion-sense when it comes to their uniforms. These outfits do not command respect, but the tone in their voices is rather clear. As I understand it this is the Gendarmerie, some French version of the National Guard, I suppose would describe it, and I guess (Sadly for them) this is their rain-gear.

Apparently this is a random inspection, and I've done nothing wrong, I think, but I can't be sure. I begin to turn on the 'ole American charm as fast as I can as I try to look straight into Mr. and Mr. Bucket-heads beady sets of eyes. How I would kill for a moment to giggle and then come back to the scene, but no such luck. They were angry now because I hadn't done as he asked... he started with hand gestures, which at first I didn't understand but luckily I caught on and turned off the car. I eek out, "Bonjour Monsieur, je ne parle pas bien votre longue," and batted my eyelashes hard. "Je suis Americane!" I've got 'em I think...

All I have told them is that I do not speak their language well and that I am an American, but it is all a ploy because I just want to get out of this mess, whatever it is. At this stage, I am shocked I could even remember the phrase. Part of it is I am not prepared for this type of incident and my vocabulary while greatly improved, isn't up on police-talk. (Vocabulary count 312) I am not ready to talk my way out of an arrest or prepared for any type of police interaction.

They rattle off their demands in the harshest French, snapping at me. Perhaps I do not have them after all. I start handing over my license (Just a guess), then the green card. They want more. The pink card is my next move. They continue to bark at me. Seems they want something else- a bribe? Why the hell didn't I listen to Philippe? Ah, the gray card. They both closely inspect every card as if I might be wanted in several countries. Time seems to be standing still. The flashlight moves from card to card and back into my face. I sit still, trying to smile while not looking creepy.

With a serious face that would kill Robocop himself, they hand me back each card and say, "Dites bonjour a Broadway pour nous." It takes me a moment to translate and it seems quite bizarre and I wonder, if I really am getting a grip on the language or not. I think they just told me to 'Give their regards to old Broadway.'

I smile, I wait, I nod and yes, that is indeed what they just said to me. I think I am going to crack up or throw up. Do you think they'd offer me their tin-helmet to puke in? It will make such a big mess of my new car otherwise.

I bat my eyelashes with all my American might and they salute me. I actually salute back... and I am on my merry way. I assume I am free to go. I am very unfamiliar with how this should go-down. I explode into laughter and continue on my way to the club. When I arrive I come to find out that there is a small search party out looking for me as I have been missing for over twenty minutes. It is comforting to know that I was missed. Me and my sweaty palms and glazed over eyes are relieved to be back amongst friends and to have the interrogation behind me.

I am ready to put myself into a self-induced state of hypnosis and I want to b-line to the bar and grab a drink. BUT- no time for that, I have to begin my hello kisses. Probably only ten new faces, on average thirty-three kisses. I'll just go through the motions and get this over with. I'm not much into the epic-greeting thing tonight, I want to tell my tin helmet Robocop story in four-part harmony, but I know, I know... first things first. To the right, *kiss*...

Friday in France

Chapter 21: Some Things Do Not Translate

French is the language that turns dirt into romance. ~ Stephen King

Drawing on my fine command of language, I said nothing.
~Anonymous

Do not- I repeat *do not* try to translate pet names, or terms of endearment. It simply doesn't work. I learned that it's best to take them at face-value; assume that the person saying them to you actually means to call you dear or darling. At least that's what I heard in my head. What was being said was;

Ma petite puce

Mon petite choux

Mon petite poulet

They all sound so damned charming; they soothed my inner ear and I couldn't help but coo at the sound of them. You may even find yourself batting your eyelashes or offering a kiss; certainly you'll feel enamored to say the least. That's until you start getting a grip on the language and you start to learn what they mean. Which for me was several months into my time here on the island. Translation:

My little flea

My little cabbage

My little chicken

It seems to me that the French simply add the word 'little' to just about anything. Magically then, the phrase transforms into pure-charm. I guess that's partly how I got here in the first place. I hear French as a magic language. I firmly believe that the French accent alone makes any word, (Understood and mostly not-understood by me,) sound incredible. It's such a smooth, poetic sounding language that just washes-over me. My little flea was one of Philippe's favorites for me. I laughed when I finally heard the translation. If truth be told, I just sort-of forced a smile when I finally understood. I didn't like it that much. Then I shared some of the more American traditional ones, I had hopes of inspiring him: Sweetheart; Sweetie; Dear; Babe or Baby.

They had some good ones you know- like *mon amour* (My love) and *mon cherrie* (My dear) but baby or dear to him was as odd as cabbage was to me. I like *ma belle* (My beautiful) and I'll get one of those every once in a while, but nine times out of ten I am a little flea. I just hope that when we visit in The States he manages to keep saying it in French instead of English because I do not know how I will explain that. Actually, I don't know why I think I'll have to explain or really who else would care. At the heart of the matter, it doesn't matter. But-being called a flea... it kind of bugs me. (Pun intended).

Between you and me, my dear reader, my *little* dear reader, it took some time to find that endearing, but once I did, I loved it.

Now, I find it totally adorable. It is all a part of the difference and finding the joy in the dissimilarity. And if I didn't want different wouldn't I be hailing a cab on 3rd Avenue on my way to meet my Baby? Yes I would, and I'm not. I believe I am all the better for it.

And being better, meant giving it my-all to learn the mother tongue. Learning French took all of my focus and living on the island kind-of propelled me into learning because no-one else spoke English really. So all day long I would engage in a solid effort to communicate. What was funny was that my skills in English quickly faded. Case in-point, when my parents would call late at night to say hello, shockingly it was difficult to think or speak in English. I am pretty sure that my Mom was thinking 'What the heck is wrong with you?' It's difficult to explain, and I am sure it seems so put-on and fake, but it wasn't. I couldn't find the words, because I spent all my time and energy and brain power to <u>not</u> think in English. Actually it was more like I just trained myself to think in French first.

Even thinking in French first, there are other things that I can't seem to get right, or get used to. For example; il pleut means, it's raining, and Je pleure means, I'm crying. So I always mix up the two; sharing, "I saw a sad movie and I *rained* through the entire film." And that, "Oh, there's a bad rain storm coming this weekend and it is supposed to *cry* all day long on Saturday." No one corrected me though, ever. To them, this was quite cute. To me, I was frustrated because I could not hear the difference between pleut and pleure and well that's where the humility comes-in when learning a new language I suppose. And humbled I was, as my vocabulary count finally started to reach-over the thousand word-mark; I still had so much more to learn.

Chapter 22: Ode to the Toilettes

France is the only country where the money falls apart and you can't tear the toilet paper. ~Billy Wilder

France cannot be France without greatness. ~Charles de Gaulle

Toilettes… toilettes… toilettes… where can I begin? So much to say and yet, so much I probably shouldn't say. As I mentioned before I am sitting on one right now, my writing headquarters. It's 4am and I am writing my notes for the day… it is that and the fact that the toilets here offer such mystery, a challenge, sort of my daily puzzle, that I must include this chapter.

None of this odd-toilette stuff should come as a big surprise because I'd been to Europe before. On my first trip to Europe several years ago I was with my friend Patty; our awe for everything new and different was tremendous. It was so new and different to us that it was a real-eye opener. The toilettes happen to be a source of amazement and confusion for us both. We had it worked out early on in our travels, that whoever went to the washroom first would report back as to what kind of WC it was. It used to determine whether or not we could stay for a long period of time or not. Needless to say (But I will anyway) the Turkish toilet, where you get to stand and do your business, guaranteed a very short visit to whatever bar or brasserie we were in, no matter how fabulous everything else was.

For some odd reason each toilet is different. Like where you flush it, how you flush it and sometimes it took longer than others to figure it out. Even though it has been four years since my first visit to France my surprise, interest and confusion over the toilettes is still very well intact. I am always amazed to see men urinate in a common area, no matter how long I travel the world. I mean shouldn't that thing be behind a wall or something. And by thing, I meant urinal… although I suppose that THING goes wherever the urinal goes.

Can we agree, a urinal should not be in plain view of the women-folk, right? No matter how long I live on this Island or on planet earth that will still be a shocker.

The fact is, is that in many fine restaurants men and women share the common area; they wash their hands at the sink together, check their hair in the mirror in the same space- and frankly, I found that awkward. Not as awkward as a urinal being right in the room with us, but – weird. I'm just not used to being in a public bathroom with a guy I don't know. I don't like fixing my make-up in front of a man, whether or not he is peeing, it made me self-conscious. I think it takes a little magic out of the dining experience.

Figuring out how to flush and where the light switch might be located, could easily be another marathon event, Olympic style. Although the European nations would dominate, win the gold and we'd still be inside the WC, looking for the chain or lever or handle.

For a beginner it takes a few minutes to master these small but oh-so-necessary details. I can remember laughing with my friend Patty and I can picture from that point forward, in my life, always wanting to report to her on the toilettes of the world. Yes, we are quite close indeed.

Of course the all-time worst is the hole in the ground- Turkish toilet. I don't even want my feet to touch those slots that are dedicated to them. And really- how are you supposed to do this? In any bathroom you want to touch as little as possible. So what is the answer? Squat? First, I have got to figure a way out to remove my underwear, (Which by the way is a very good reason to just go without a.k.a. commando) but in those days, I didn't and even if I did I still lacked the balancing skills to pull the rest of it off. For argument sake though, let's say that if you are wearing a skirt, which would be a great advantage at this point, that will only get you a slight leg-up (So to speak).

It still takes dedication and agility and probably several years of gymnastic training, minimally a limber body, just to get the underwear off. Forget about wearing jeans –really-- trying this, must be reserved for gold-metal winners only. Now to add one more complication- half of these bathrooms don't have latches that are in working order. So how you are suppose-to balance yourself, AND keep the door shut with one hand, remove your underwear and pee? I used to think I was good at multitasking before I was up for this challenge. No, I can admit defeat. My ego is simply not that large and my sights are not set that high. Nope, my plan is to establish what kind of bathroom is in the place and then I either drink or not, and plan my departure time accordingly. Actually due to the toilette situation I probably did more barhopping and restaurant hopping in Europe than anywhere else. Not in search of a good time, but a good commode. What a drag though, because there were times that you could be having a blast and yet, you'd have to leave, you'd just have to. Something's wrong with that. And really- how can a nice restaurant anywhere, consider having a standing toilet?

Regardless, my time on the Island reinforced my amusement with toilettes. I've been relieved (Pun intended) every time I find a reasonably normal situation. The other toilet that I find difficult to warm-up to is... the seat-less version. What is that, why is that? I mean the seat doesn't do much, granted, but is something I guess I've become accustomed to and I just want one, be it made of their thin plastic or real porcelain. The thin plastic isn't comforting at all either and it slides easily too, especially if you're trying not to really touch it. Blech.

Months after I've been on the Island I still want a toilet seat, and if I have my choice it is porcelain, for sure. For a gal who wants change in her life, some old habits die hard.

I have noticed I have evolved some... I don't jump or twitch gracelessly when I see a man urinating next to me, although I still try to avoid eye contact, and of course I try not to do a hood/no-hood random inspection by accident. After running into my share of men at the urinal in France I find myself with a new-found gratitude that there is no girl-to-guy hand shaking in this country as well.

Go ahead, pee next to me... I mean sure, whip out your hooded or non-hooded penis and take a pee. What the hell. It doesn't exactly say bon appetite to me, but I can fight the urge to run away laughing. See? I've evolved.

Chapter 23: The Felix Unger of France

Life is not measured by the number of breaths we take but by the moments that take our breath away. ~Anonymous

We need not think alike to love alike. ~Frances David

I'm not sure how French this is or if this is a particular Philippe thing, but he is the Felix Unger of France, and I may not be Oscar, but we are an odd couple to be sure. The man actually follows me around the house with a broom. Is this OCD or just YGTBKM? (You've Got To Be KIDDING ME.) He folds shirts to perfection (Good to know he can rely on a job at the Gap if we return to The States). He adjusts the curtains for optimal placement so that a streak of sun will shine through and yet at night a car light will not be too jarring. His shoes must be organized along the wall, blue high top sneakers come before the white ones, and it goes from there, each having their place. Am I the only one that is not organized this way?

The helmet to the BMW must be hung on the wall on its assigned hook, which should not be confused with the hook assigned for his jean jacket or his wet suit. Please people, we need to keep order here! And by people, I mean me... because I am anything but methodical about where things go.

The fact that the stereo speaker must be at a ninety-degree angle, is beyond my comprehension. And my guess is if you are staying in a house on Fire Island, things are wildly less than organized. (Unless Philippe is visiting)

Every morning after his shower he hangs the bathroom mat on the close-line to air it out, of course it is returned promptly at 3pm for the afternoon shower session. Yes, I met a Frenchmen who showers not once but twice a day... so we can all agree he is not typically French after all. Cleaning my hairbrush is now and extra burden he must carry because I certainly could care less. And that is a feeling that I have regardless of where I am on the planet. Of course toothpaste caps must be firmly attached and the tube must be evenly distributed and rolled properly.

My fear over the French Food God has been replaced by fear of Philippe. I'm what people call a 'creative' and creative types tend not to be OCD or uptight about any of this kind of stuff. If I could I would, but I can't and I won't be obsessed over that kind of a thing. That would leave very little time to worry about toilettes and kisses and open-air-boobs. Clearly, those are my obsessions of choice.

Sometimes I can get him to relax, we'll hang out lazily in our hammock in the garden, and I'll forget how crazy he is about his neatness. And at that very moment he can forgive my sloppiness. I suppose whatever language your relationship takes place in, someone has got to be the Yin to your Yang. OK so maybe not this extreme, put the broom down for Christ sake, at least until I finish making a mess.

See to me, when I fall in love, I don't see the irritations, the OCD or whatever. I actually enjoy doing the laundry and washing the floors... and believe me, I think that was a once in a life time thing for me. I mean, I never want to wash floors again. I'm a serious career girl temporarily without a career, so to speak. But with or without a career, I tend to be without the desire to wash a floor. So I am trying to be open to everything that is here for me, including the Felix of France. Don't worry my clothes are still on the floor from time to time, I'm just trying to make it as reasonable for both of us as possible; small piles in the corner of the room should work.

Even when my clothes aren't on the floor I am noticing that they are getting moldy. Apparently this is an issue related to living in a home that is 300-500 years old that is made of old stone and lacks air-conditioning or air-flow of any kind. This is a new problem for me and I am not really sure how to manage it. I don't think there is a dry-cleaner on the Island and I am not sure what alternate remedies might work. My beautiful Betsey Johnson clothes have mold on them. Philippe, being the Mr. Clean that he is says to wash it off on a sunny day and hang them on the line. He tells me I'll get used to it. This- I doubt.

Chapter 24: Lucid Dreams

Do not spoil what you have by desiring what you have not; remember that what you now have was once among the things you only hoped for. ~Epicurus

Dreams are like stars...you may never touch them, but if you follow them they will lead you to your destiny. ~Anonymous

Walking through our neighbor's wine-field one day it struck me that I had long ago wished for a life as exotic as this. Living in Europe, being in love, I had always wanted to experience a completely different world. Now as I sauntered past the grape vines I looked at them differently. I started to really take in what my life had become and even wondered if I had created it through my incessant daydreaming. It seemed quite dreamlike now, bizarre; perhaps I had actually found what I had dreamt about; it all had a sense of déjà vu about it.

I examined my life here more closely; it was the life I had always thought about and now I was living it. When I was daydreaming at work at CNBC I had no idea that it would actually play out, manifest itself, but I knew that I wanted something. Of course I had visualized myself as a very thin version of me, and that part had finally come true. Yeah me! (Take that FFG!) But beyond that, what I was living felt familiar and new and funny and surreal all at once. I almost wanted to pinch myself. Here I am, living in Europe, I was in love, and I was so happy, not working, not worrying. Just, watching my life unfold, it was charmed.

If flowers can pop up overnight, if my boobs have super-hero powers, and if I can speak French, it must be magic. It was so glorious and strange it was otherworldly, out of the ordinary certainly for me, a city slicker, and yet it was so me.

I had wanted to live a life that was so remote from what I had known, I had wanted to experience the polar-opposite of what I knew and what I had lived in New York City, and I was actually doing it. For some reason, even though I spent my time constantly observing the differences, I failed to see how far I had come. I can picture myself running down the hall with tape in my hand at CNBC thinking, 'can't do this forever.'

It was as if my daydreams had come to life. My ideas and musings had jumped out from my mind and leapt out into an alternate existence and in living color. It was a fairytale filled with all the enchantment and charm a girl could want. The fact that I was now walking through this lucid dream, step by step was powerful and all consuming. It was almost difficult to recall the life I had left behind, but believe me... New York takes some real time, and real effort to just fade from memory, that is for sure.

I certainly miss my friends and family. I totally miss a good rotisserie chicken and a frozen margarita and some nights I even miss that feeling of being pushed around, or that sense of running late. But I get over it, nine times out of ten because that is what four out of five dentists would want for me.

Chapter 25: Halloween

The important thing is this: To be able at any moment to sacrifice what we are for what we could become. ~*Charles Dubois*

Barbara and I have set up an art studio on their property in their guest cottage and now that the summer has passed, and the season is over, we spend a lot of time painting furniture that we will later sell in various gift shops. I love it. It is the best thing for both of us. I also need to start feeling like I am doing something useful as I am getting antsy. Spending my days exercising or hanging on the beach or even babysitting her boys, is just not enough. Doing the art work together feels great and as the last of the warm days fade and fall is upon us. I feel more committed to being here. Working toward my future here and having a fantastic art studio and great friend and artist to pass my time with really helps ground me and give me energy. We even talk of maybe opening our own gallery, gift shop if things go well.

Minimally, we are two creative people who spend our days together laughing and talking and having some creative outlet. Since I have been on the Island for a while now, this becomes part of my new routine. And visiting with her kids and eating dinner with them is also a big part of my life.

On occasion I'd pick up the kids at school and take them for a treat. On one of those days, I went to get Raphael first, as his class let out several minutes before his brothers. Raphael came out waving happily, with a smile from ear to ear and his coat opened wide. I leaned down to kiss him hello, and to button up his jacket. I was eye level with him, kneeling on the cobblestone, when he suddenly grabbed my face. He cupped my chin using his tiny hands, forcing my eyes to meet his. Then he said, "Te belle Judith!" To this day, I don't know how I didn't melt on the spot.

Whenever I was with the boys I'd tell them all sorts of stories about the U.S.A. and they would eat them up, hungry for more. They want to know everything about real American kids and what they do. I tell them about hot-dogs and apple-pie, I'd make them grilled cheese sandwiches with milkshakes and they think I am the best cook and the best storyteller of all time. They would listen as if I have just revealed some stellar state-secrets. I recount stories about campfires and s'mores, baseball and roller coasters. Of course, I mention Halloween which is only a few weeks away now. I wanted to hear about what costumes they are planning on-the regular stuff; I was assuming they have their own version. They listen, but they are in shock, I can tell they really do not believe me. "C'est pas vrai, Judith" says Raphael. And I say, "Yes it is true...indeed it is, kids go door to door and say trick or treat and get bags full of candy."

Nicolas listens and laughs, thinking I am really just pulling their legs. I am surprised they don't believe me and they are surprised that I think they are so gullible. Nicolas is the older brother and warns Raphael that this is some sort of joke. This sounds larger than life and completely hilarious to them. I assure them, it is true and that North American kids would be shocked to hear that they do not have the same holiday! It takes some time and a lot of convincing, but they finally believe me.

We sit at the dinner table practicing the phrase "Trick or treat" and we all have a good laugh. You have to hear it with a super-strong French accent to understand how sweet it is. I say, we have got to celebrate, I mean, every kid has the right to have Halloween. What a gift to be the person to introduce them that! So the boys decide that they will make their own costumes and this will take weeks of planning and hard work and I begin the search for a pumpkin.

I search high and low and there are no pumpkins to be had. Believe me, I went to farmer's markets and grocery stores, but I finally ended up with some kind of squash, actually several squash varieties. It worked out fine, as they obviously didn't know the difference. So we carved our first, squash together and we make Jack-o-lanterns. We place the candles in and with the flick of a match we light up the room. The light not only shines from glow cast by the flame, but also from these two very shiny, very happy faces. Our excitement for Halloween increases exponentially.

I go to the store and buy a bunch of candy, after all I am going to be the one-and-only house they can come to and trick or treat at. I'd say I bought like ten regular size candy bars each (Because there is no such thing as Halloween size of course) and a bunch of smaller items, looking in the bag it didn't seem like that much, but it would have to do. Barbara is probably going to kill me, they just aren't accustomed to encouraging their kids to pig-out on candy. For the days that remained the boys worked diligently on their costumes. They would give me daily updates. But, I was not allowed to see them; this was their surprise and gift for me.

Finally the day was upon us and I was in the art-studio guest cottage painting, awaiting the boy's arrival. We had one last rehearsal and went over the most important line, 'Trick or treat' and what to do next, and how to approach the door. They were so excited, I was afraid it would not be nearly as thrilling as it need-be. With so much preparation time and ramping up for it- I was concerned it would be a huge letdown. The boys went to go get in to their costumes and I went to go light several of the jack-o-lanterns so that they would be burning on the studio steps. They had been instructed to only go to houses that had Jacko-lanterns lit. The studio-cottage would be the only one welcoming trick-or-treaters, on the entire continent.

I could hear the giggles long before I heard the knock on the door, and I answered, they yelled (Well, as loud as two French kids can yell) "Trick or Treat Judith!" I stood at the open door with my jaw agape. I was so impressed with their costumes and I went on and on about how fabulous they were. They really were amazing. They worked so hard on them, masks and all. I don't know exactly what they were; they looked like young princes' at a renaissance-ball with their hand held feathered face masks to add to their costumes, and they were stunning! They had spent hours upon hours making them, just for this moment.

I handed over the bags of candy and the boys looked in, looked in again and beamed. They kissed me (Once to the right-*kiss*, to the left *kiss*!) and then looked back into the bag. They were so excited that they kissed me again! Obviously breaking any and all kissing rules. I was glowing! They looked like they had won the lottery. We stood around and laughed and practiced the 'Trick or treat' phrase; which is tough on the French accent, so that they could make sure they had it right to tell their friends about it at school the next day. We sat in the cottage-studio and they each ate one candy bar. SO not-American.

For months afterwards, they would take me into their room and show me what candy they had left of their stash. Reviewing what they had eaten, what they hadn't. They savored it, every morsel, and not just the candy either, but the entire experience. It was one of the best Halloweens I ever had. And when I tell you that they talked about Halloween for years to come, believe me, I'm not exaggerating.

Chapter 26: Goodbye Gift

They're funny things, accidents. You never have them till you're having them. ~Alan Alexander Milne

Humor is a serious thing. I like to think of it as one of our greatest earliest natural resources, which must be preserved at all costs. ~James Thurber

The high-season has long since passed and the Island has decreased its population from 200,000 back to 10,000, or so. It seems like the Island is resting, recuperating, deflated a bit; everything seems to be back where it used to be, before August 1st. There are a few stragglers though; the weather is still pleasant too. School has been in session for months so it is mostly elderly tourists who linger or those away for a weekend jaunt. It is very quiet and serene.

It was probably about 10pm and Philippe was going to finish work within a half hour or so, I just didn't feel like waiting around the restaurant. I figured I'd go home and paint for a while or read. So I began cruising down the Route National on my way. It is pitch black and warm outside, a welcome silence washed over me from my vantage point inside my little Renault. I found that I wasn't even aware of shifting gears anymore. I had become entirely accustomed to driving a stick shift. Perhaps I didn't do it exceptionally well, but at least I didn't strip the gears or bypass any of them. And I admit, I am quite satisfied and proud to announce that I do remember to release the emergency break before I get-going.

The Island was quiet, quieter than normal probably due to the earlier rain. I don't know what it was but I was so peaceful in this little car, on my way home. I was just really ready to be alone for a few moments, happy to be on my way to our humble abode and get cozy in our tiny dwelling and maybe call my folks to say hello.

Suddenly a fox ran out in front of me onto the pavement that was still slick. I reacted quickly. But I am certain I over-reacted. Years of driving in Manhattan had not prepared me for a random fox in the road. I swerved the wheel to the right, which had him change his path and then I pulled quickly to the left. I must have over adjusted the steering wheel because the harsh, wild tug on the wheel had the car spinning on the open road. As the car was spiraling I remember grabbing on.

To say my life flashed before me may seem like a bit of a cliché but I was curious if Philippe would even know how to contact my parents and inform them of my death. Did he know where I kept my passport? Would he have to contact The U.S. Consulate or would he make Barbara, the best English-speaker on the Island, share the sad news with my parents? Would Gregory be a close runner up, since his English had improved over the past-few months? Really, we never discussed dying. We were just started to live together. Death wasn't on my mind... not until the car began to take its second 360 spin.

I knew I had to steady my body. The road was only two lanes and I was flying across both of them. On-coming traffic be-damned, or the fox should certainly be damned, I could not stop the car from spinning. I braced for the worst, and some-how, during that time when things slow to a pace where your brain has plenty of time to absorb what is happening, I thought, why now? I'm so happy...

I could feel myself being lifted from the seat itself. My shoulders were stiff and I held-tight as if it would help as I knew a huge smash was sure to be next. The end of my life, as I knew it, was approaching.

The car spun so many times that it actually took flight and I ended up on the other side of the road, in a wine-field, facing the direction I had just come from. I landed, amazed that I didn't hit oncoming traffic, absolutely amazing.

It took me a moment to wrap my shook-up-brain-around what just happened. I was now facing the direction I came from but I was at least fifty feet off of the road. I took a deep breath. Inhale, exhale, (Let me try that again) inhale, exhale... I seem to be able to manage the basics of breathing, so that's a good sign.

Perhaps the French Food God had finally started taking notice of my diligent starvation tactics, because something, some-force greater than I, intervened. I should be dead. Remind me to eat rabbit tomorrow, my final-food frontier, just my way of saying thanks for my survival.

Normally at this time of night there would be several cars on the road, but for that flash in time, it was just me, the road, and the fox. Now it was just me, and the wine field. God knows where the fucking fox was. It was so quiet when the car landed. Quiet, still, dead-silence... an entirely new level of stillness, I was not yet accustomed to. By the way, 'landed' is not necessarily a word I would like to use in a sentence when describing a drive home.

Anyway, I was off the road and it was off-season, and a remarkably quiet night, or at least quiet for a few moments. I sat. I clung to the steering wheel as if it could ground me. I needed to let go but my fingers were unaware of my brain's desire. The shock of the moment began to lift and the gratitude I felt moved into the stillness and silence of the night. I was quite lucky.

I was startled and relieved all at once. How was it that I hadn't been hit? How am I alive? I sat there for a minute or two while I let my brain catch up to me. The slow motion thing had stopped it was just my brain that was slow and I spent a moment reliving the accident. It was then that my (former) life in NY flashed before me, a sort-of a delayed, mini-review. Everything seemed fine though, enough to bring my brain back to the present-tense. And so I managed to find myself once again in attendance, here in the field. For some reason I kept looking for the fox, as if that mattered.

As noted, the car was actually facing the opposite direction, but it seemed OK, except for the fact that it had stopped running, I guess at the time of the landing. That was my initial assessment anyway. I could see the road, although I seemed to be a few feet lower than it. I thought it might be a bit tricky to drive it out of here. Of course it was pitch black, darker than dark-because there aren't really any streetlights around and for whatever reason… there wasn't a car insight.

I tried to start the car and simply drive it out of there. No-one would have to know and I was just going to act like nothing happened. Mind you, I hadn't really looked for the best route to take out of the wine field, but I must have been in shock and so I just kept trying to start the car. The idea being I'd just kind of dust myself off and get back on the road. Unfortunately, I realized the car wasn't really in the mood to go along with my plan. So my new plan; I'd be better off to get out and walk back to the restaurant, admit to Philippe what happened and have him help me get the car out.

Damn-it though… he is going to be pissed off and I really wanted to avoid that. Any guy that likes his shoes arranged in order is probably not going to take kindly to me parking the car in a wine field. Merde! I gave the car another try… I didn't understand why it wouldn't start. Shit… I was going to have to go get him. I was worried about what he'd say, and how frickin' mad he'd be.

I suppose on the scale of one to ten, one- being him not-liking how I drive a stick-shift, this would be—a solid ten. Very much on the far side of the scale; in his finicky, wildly-picky manner, he was going to be mad. The more I let myself think about it the more I realized that for someone like Philippe who liked everything 'just so' this was definitely worse than not properly squeezing the toothpaste.

I shook it off. Or I somehow took my panic with me, because at the end of the day, I had no choice. I went into New Yorker mode. Yup, after months on the Island the old city gal kicked into gear. Ah here she is. I can handle whatever comes my way. I've got adrenaline ripping through my body; damn-it and while I see no evidence of physical injury I'm ready to take a verbal beating from Philippe. The rush of fear, relief and panic running through my veins- reminded me in an odd way of a New York minute. Anyway, I'm not afraid of him, (sort-of) and I don't care about his reaction (well maybe a little). I got out of the car and headed toward the road.

When I realized I was about two miles from the restaurant, I began to hitch. Luckily a couple of farmers picked me up. I didn't know them, I am sure they knew all about me though. And as soon as I opened my mouth, despite the fact that my accent was quite good by now, (Vocabulary count – finally, too high to count) they'd know right away that I was the famous American. For a moment all I could think about was tomorrow's farmer-gentleman's report; the crazy New Yorker smashes the car into a wine field. This should make for some fun farmer headline news for tomorrow. I put those thoughts aside so I could smile and say hello. I actually crawled into their teeny-tiny car and smooshed myself into the backseat next to several cages filled with chickens. I was a little surprised. Barely enough room for all of us, but they were there first.

Sitting next to chickens on any other night, might have really struck me as a cute Island moment. In New York the only chickens that I ever got close to were already in rotisserie form. I was too nervous about Philippe to worry about my previous chicken experiences, or lack there-of, or about being pecked to death.

Regardless, I moved as far away from the chickens as possible while I focused on my gratitude for the farmers' hospitality. I was grateful that they were willing to pick up a hitchhiker. And of course, grateful for the fact that I can pin myself up-against the non-chicken side of the backseat, out of 'pecking-range,' which makes this all very manageable. In fact, I felt that they had a-certain compassion for me (the farmers, not the chickens). I think they felt sorry for me and I sensed that there was no real judgment towards me either. Shit happens. This is the closest the farmers had gotten to me, and I to them. At least they had perfect timing. In the two minutes it took to get me to Le Forum. Along the way, I told them what happened, they nodded accordingly. Then they delivered me safely to the restaurant and wished me good luck.

Unfortunately, when I arrived I realized that my Philippe had already begun the trip home, and was probably at that exact moment driving past that area. Jesus, I was hoping he didn't see the car off the road. I was hopeful that the dark Island night was working in my favor.

The owner of the restaurant and our good friend, Philippe, was surprised to see me return to the restaurant as well. Once he did see me, he knew something was wrong; I was apparently shaking from head to toe. He knew my late visit wasn't expected and I guess the shaking, stunned look were good solid hints. He offered me a big glass of wine, which I tilted back pretty quickly. Then he gave me a lift back to the scene of the crime. He told me not to worry, everything would be fine. I didn't believe him, but I welcomed hearing it anyway.

When we got to the car to take a look, he pointed out that all of the wheels were actually sticking out, sort of flat and perpendicular to the car. That's the best description I can come up with is – sort-of cartoon like. I suppose that would be the best account, except it lacked the comedy, or animation but, it certainly had the visual punch. Even I could tell that this was not a good sign; how'd I miss that before? It certainly didn't bode well for the easy removal of the auto as I had hoped. The car must have taken flight even more than I thought. I guess in the moment I didn't realize how hard the landing actually was. Thank goodness (I suppose) that the soft mud of the wine field broke the fall. My poor, little, dear, new (to me) hatchback Renault. I hope that fox lives a long and healthy life.

Both Philippe and I began to worry about my Philippe's reaction when he got home to an empty house. So we drove out to our t-tiny house and found Philippe there, His face was crinkled and he had a furrow in his brow. I told him what happened, right away. It was kind of like ripping a Band-Aid off, quick, painful but it was done. He knew something was up before I arrived anyway and I think he was mostly relieved to find me safe. (Mostly) Deep down, I am sure he was super-pissed. I also think that when you start to worry and you start to think that you may have almost just lost the one you love, you shut up and save the yelling at that particular loved-one for later.

All three of us got into the mini-van and headed back to the car, out there in the wine-field. There it sat, with its little tires pushed out, pressed into the mud. My little car looked sad out in the dark night, misplaced among the grapes. My two concerned looking Philippes quickly and easily assessed and agreed (Somehow) that the car was dead. I just looked on and pretended that I couldn't understand a word of French. This was a moment to take advantage of. For a long instant I felt like a big heel, a big stupid heel.... although I know it was an accident.

Really I was so lucky that I hadn't been injured or didn't hurt anyone else, that when all's said and done, the car seemed secondary. I couldn't take back the accident and I couldn't repair the car.

We had to leave the car there overnight and my Philippe would deal with it at day-break. So much for our plans to hit the beach tomorrow. He is pissed. I know he's pissed and I'm really sorry if that counts for anything. My Philippe doesn't say much, we drive back to our house, a long –reasonably quiet ride home. He does though, take his hand off of the stick shift and reach for mine and give me a tight squeeze.

The next day I walked into the restaurant, the Chef who had given us (Me) the car was so kind. He was gracious and quite funny. He simply applauded when I walked in. Actually, the entire kitchen staff applauded, and I took my bow.

I was the source of many good jokes... that is for sure. Actually, I apologized profusely to the Chef, and he told me that it was my car to trash, and he smiled and let me know he was relieved that I was OK.

My Philippe heard through 'the grape-vine' (pun-intended) that the farmers were all a buzz. Big news, lots of chatter for the bored farmers today, something about a fox, a wine-field, a Renault and an American; he was expecting it but, I am sure, it didn't help.

I think they even named a fox-animal-rights group after me at some point. But no-one was really upset, only relieved, and happy I was alright. The Chef, Daniel, made it really clear, he made sure I knew that he was not mad at all, as he knew I was having a bit of a hard time forgiving myself. He said he was content and grateful that I got some use out of the car before I smashed it in the wine-field. He was genuinely pleased that it served us well. (Sincerity intended) He was so kind and considerate and for him, it was a great source of comedy. Philippe (my Philippe) managed to bite his tongue, even though I know that if he could have he would have offered me another driving lesson.

Rule #2; no mention of wine fields or foxes. (Not necessarily in that order).

Besides, my punishment was already lined up and waiting for me and I have no one to blame but myself (or the fox); I'm back to driving the mini-van again.

Chapter 27: I Think I Do!

The longest journey a man must take is the eighteen inches from his head to his heart. ~Anonymous

If you don't know where you are going, any road will get you there. ~Lewis Carroll

Winter on the Island is a completely different experience. Long gone are the tourists, and the core people that remain- the shopkeepers and restaurant owners are the ones that are left to keep up the momentum and spirit of the place. Many people close their shops and go on holiday themselves. It is grey and oddly much slower and quieter and sometimes a little sad. The best part is, I feel like a true local and there is an intimacy and sense of belonging that warms my spirit. It seems like light-years have passed since we basked openly in the French sun. Walks on the beach are nice, and the surfers continue to give it a go in their wetsuits but the beach is no longer headquarters for a social life. *My bad-boys* are behind fleece and many layers of clothes, and even sometimes a leather coat; I am constantly cold.

The air has a bite to it even though the temperature rarely drops below the low fifties. There is a chill here that for some is a welcome change. For others it casts a melancholy mood that matches the earlier sunset of the winter solstice. Being at sea level creates a unique dampness from the salty sea air that reaches deep in my bones. I now realize that the wood-burning stove is not a piece of art, rather my new best friend; it is the only heat we have in our entire baby house. Philippe actually chops the wood himself to keep the flames going. He goes out to the garden and hacks at wood and in some very primal way, provides for me. I like to sit on the woodstove which Philippe finds disturbing. I find it the only time I feel toasty, and I like the sensation of almost burning my legs through my worn out jeans. The thing is there aren't many places that are heated well. Even if they are heated with some newer type of appliance the majority of buildings here were built in the 16th through the 19th Century so they don't hold much of the heat for long. The warmth provided by furnaces, fireplaces and stone-hearths slips away effortlessly through the stone walls and back out to the Island itself. For months I feel as though I can never truly warm up, and I long for a bathtub to soak my bones. Every once in a while we'll get a very sunny day and it will help to heat my body, but other than that, I am typically consuming firewood faster than Philippe can chop.

Since season is past, he isn't working as many hours now so we have time to hang out together and he has time to take me around the Island. We visit some of the sites together. We hit the Citadel, which I had been to myself over the summer in The Château; a complex fortification built in many stages over 120 year period. I am sure it served its purpose back in the 16th century but now it is just part of another magical village to discover and enjoy together. It's like everything else in France, the village streets, the churches- castles, forts, tons of history everywhere and I think when you live there you can easily take it for granted. Philippe has a chance to enjoy it through my eyes and he takes time to tell me about the places that we are visiting. He has become my roving-reference librarian. This is much better for me, than carrying around a history book.

We travel to Fort Boyárd which has a glorious history dating back to the 17th Century, when there was a greater need for military protection. Apparently the construction was quite difficult; (This might be a slight understatement) it took almost two hundred years for it to be finished. Many leaders gave up on it including Napoleon-Bonaparte. The funny thing is, is that in recent history it has been made popular by some crazy TV show, and everyone on the Island is more excited about its recent claim to fame then the really cool history itself. Finally, under the reign of Louis Philippe it was completed. Figures- a guy named Philippe would be involved.

Of course I went with him to Saint-Denis at the other end of the Island, because in the winter the surf was better there. He would surf and I would explore. I walked around and discovered a 12th Century church with an amazing façade. It appears that there are many churches, at least one in each village and even churches that date back to the 11th Century, such as Saint-George's church. We go everywhere spending a lot of time together, to lunch, to visit friends. The winter is much slower but I have Philippe to share it with so despite the cold air and closed-up shops, I am very content.

We spend a lot of time in our little house, talking, laughing and making- love. One afternoon we were hanging out in our damp bedroom, passing time together before he had to go to the dentist and then to work. The air was crisp and we cuddled for warmth, I think Philippe was getting tired of cutting so much firewood. We were talking about how I have to leave in late January for a bit in order to keep my tourist visa legal and all. Somewhere along the conversation we start talking about my paper work and all of that logistical stuff that I hate. I ask him if he will come to The States with me this trip to meet my family and see my life. I'm afraid he has fallen in love with only one tiny part of me...and really hasn't seen me in my environment. He talks about since we are going to spend our lives together anyway why not just get married now so we don't have to deal with that hassle anymore. He doesn't hesitate and then (If memory serves) he mutters something like, "OK, New York, Buffalo and then we'll marry after that."

"Oh," he looks at his watch, he's got to fly if he is going to get to the dentist on time or not. He kisses me and leaves, and says, "Are you coming to the restaurant tonight?" I am certain I looked confused when I replied, "Not sure, I have stuff I want to get done, if I'm not there by 9pm then I am not coming and I'll just see you here later." Thinking, I'll be the one sitting here reviewing every word of our last conversation and wondering if you just asked me to marry you.

He walks out the door and I dial my sister Donna as quickly as I can. "Hey listen, you can't tell anyone this, but I think Philippe just asked me to marry him." Of course she wanted to know how I wasn't exactly sure about that. She says, "What do you mean you don't know – how aren't you sure if he proposed or not?"

And so for an $80-evaluation we went over each word, item by item. Yup, she agreed, sounds like you might be engaged, but neither one of us would bet the farm on it. I called my friend Mary and then my friend Patty to over-analyze the same conversation. We all were somewhere between excited and confused. I mean, there was no ring, no nothing, not even a 'Will you marry me?' not in French or in English. I hung up the last call and continued to review it in my head.

The trick with Philippe is that, he always knew we would be together from the first moment we met. He assumed we would spend our lives together, always. For him, there never was a need for formalities and questions, proposals and such.

That wasn't me and or my style. I never assumed that, even at this point in time. To him though, there was nothing to analyze, nothing to figure out, it just was.

For me, as time went on and we talked as if we were a life-long couple, I still didn't know that to be true. He wanted to have kids right away, and I wanted to figure out where we would live and all of that. So it wasn't so far-off that he would propose because we did talk about our future and our lives together. But it would be more official, and real, if he had. Did he?

When he walked through the door later that night, I summoned my courage and asked him, in my best French. I danced around it a bit, but I was going to scream it out one way or the other, there was no way I could hold back. The basic essence of the conversation that night was, "Hey-did you ask me to marry you or what?" He laughed, "Of course, I always have." (What?) What does that mean? I always have. But I knew, he had thought of us as married from the moment that I moved in.

OK but I still want to know was that proposal for real, I mean, can we go get a ring or something, are we officially engaged? Most young French people just live together these days, and he probably would have done that too, if it weren't for the international complications and need for paper work. Not that he didn't see us as husband and wife, he did. He saw us as a couple all-along, to him- I was his wife, his life partner.

The next day we went to La Rochelle, the very same lovely port city where the train station was. It was also the place that one would go to do real shopping. I didn't want an expensive ring, nor did I want a diamond. I wanted something colorful that would represent us, and our uniqueness. I saw a sparkly blue topaz framed by two sapphires and it was unique enough and bright enough and just odd enough to be perfect enough. He wouldn't let me wear it out of the store. Instead that night at a friend's house he tells the story of his non-proposal, and my 'when can we go get a ring?' part in it, and then says to them; (I'll translate) "With you as our witness, I would like to officially ask Judith to marry me."

We drank champagne and laughed and as soon as the time change allowed, I called my parents and my sisters to tell them the official-news. It was kind of odd, because they hadn't met this man that I lived with, they didn't know him, but they all congratulated us. Their excitement for our trip home escalated, and also turned into a wedding planning trip. We would have a big wedding in

Buffalo the following fall, with my family, and hopefully some of our friends would make the trip from France as well.

Somewhere between our trip to Buffalo and New York to meet my friends and family I guess I expected him to freak. But he didn't, it all went exceptionally well. He had been to The States before and loved the voyage. He was after all a real traveler at heart, and he loved me regardless of what continent I was on. He got along exceptionally well with everyone, although I am sure there were some that wondered how a high powered TV Executive would live happily ever after with a French-Surfer.

Someone recommended that we just check in and meet with a lawyer regarding the paperwork we may or may-not need, we did. The NY immigration attorney informed us that we really should get married in France and pronto, or I'd be kicked out of the country. That was a bit of a shocker.

We literally had to digest this information on the flight home because we met with the lawyer in New York City the very last day before we left. We had bought wedding rings and everything and had left them in Buffalo for our future-fall wedding. Now what? We decided that for paper-work sake we would have a French wedding (So that I could stay legally) and then go ahead with the big family wedding later on. While my family understood, they were hurt on some level (For that I will always be sorry) and believe me it was a weird concept to have a makeshift wedding on the Island without any family present.

We decided to roll with it and not get too hung up on anything, we didn't have much of a choice. We'd exchange the rings in Buffalo at the family affair and exchange the legal-vows in France. For me it was just another exercise in not knowing what the hell was going on.

In France, you have to be married by the Mayor of the town where you live. So the first step is meeting with the Mayor and offering up many family facts and just piles of information. If you want a religious ceremony you can do that after, in our case, we just wanted to get this part done so we could live without fear of me being deported.

Next you have to have blood tests and post an advertisement in the paper for thirty days announcing your intentions of marrying so that if either one of you are already married, witnesses can come forward and stop the charade. (It's true). We went through the blood tests and the print-up in the paper and we ran around getting the proper papers required in order. The French love bureaucratic bullshit sponsored by paperwork and red-tape, a wedding was a perfect occasion for all of that. I followed Philippe's lead.

I could feel spring in the air and the Island while still cold and crisp finally offered more sun. I love when the days get longer, it makes me feel like world is opening up again. There was an increase in light, a bright glow and a-certain luminosity that only spring could bring. The balance of the brightness I feel, must be related to our upcoming nuptials.

Meanwhile my friend Barbara offered up 'Le Transat' Night Club as a space for the wedding which was now scheduled for April 1, at 3pm.

Why 3pm? Because in France everyone works such off hours with breaks in the middle. If you worked at a restaurant you would be off from 3-6pm but if you owned a store, you would be off from 12n-3pm we figured this way, most people could be either late to return to work or late to arrive to our wedding. Those who wanted to be there, could.

Barbara also offered to make some tapas, and we said we'd buy a few cases of champagne. We told people to feel free to come in jeans- it was casual, it was simple. As they day got closer my American friends and family felt like they lived farther and farther away. So far away and I could feel the sadness. The distance seemed extreme and I tried to push down the sadness. I reminded them that the real wedding was in Buffalo and that I loved them.

The only other person that was upset about our pending marriage… was Raphael. He couldn't understand how I could go off and marry Philippe, when he was clearly there waiting. Although my French was much better now, it was still difficult for me to find the words, to explain myself to Raphael. I did my very best to let him know just how special he'd always be to me. I asked his mom, Barbara, to stand up for me and also to tell me what the hell was going on because I had never been to one wedding in France. So mine, would be my first. I had my suspicion that this would be another cultural learning opportunity. I didn't know if I was to say, I do, I will, or what. In fact, she said we would be seated for most of it so she could tap me under that table if I wasn't responding correctly. Already I'm confused—seated? Table?

The day came, the Mayor read this very long list of facts about who are parents were, where they were, including their addresses and we stood in front of probably twenty friends. I do remember when the Mayor said the part about kissing the bride - we kissed. At that moment more friends piled in (Of course they had just gotten off of work) so the Mayor who had a nice sense of style decided to repeat the kissing the bride part again for those who had just arrived. We kissed and everyone clapped, and we piled out of the Mayor's office with a flowering plant that the town of Dolus, the 'mother-town' to our village of Le Deux, gave us as our first wedding gift. And then we made our way a kilometer down the road to Le Transat where about thirty friends gathered and drank champagne.

The Chef and his wife and eight month old son Valentine were in attendance, as were Gregory and Laurence, Nicolas and Raphael, and Steph, as well as, Philippe the owner of the restaurant and so on and so on. It was a great party. When it ended about three hours later, Gregory and Laurence invited the remaining twenty people back to their house for an apéritif. We stayed there, eating small amounts of weird chips and olives. And after that about ten of us, who were still standing, went to a fancy restaurant, for a nice sit down dinner. All of that was just off the cuff and lots of fun. It was so casual and relaxed, it really was fun to be at a wedding with people in jeans and no throwing of flowers and no garter belts etc. I don't remember even having any wedding cake-but that we would do in Buffalo, later, for the big wedding. This was just a small wedding, for legal reasons.

But in all actuality, it was the real deal. I didn't even get that myself, until maybe a year or so later when it came time to celebrate our first anniversary. From that point on we celebrated both anniversaries. However there was something so poignant about getting married on the Island. For me it was almost a mini graduation, from city-gal to fake-Frenchie and I adored every last second of it. It really was the coolest wedding ever. A bunch of surfers, some champagne and one formerly crazed New York TV producer, currently calm… saying I do to her very own Philippe… it was perfect.

Friday in France

Chapter 28: Strange, But True

If you must sleep through a third of your life, why should you sleep through your dreams, too? ~Stephen LaBerge

All journeys have secret destinations of which the traveler is unaware. ~Martin Buber

I got up today and had a long walk to the beach. I walked up and down the empty sandy shores enjoying the crisp air. On the way home I picked up a baguette, shoved it under my arm tearing off warm little pieces as I walked through the vineyards. I nodded a little hello to the roosters as I passed our neighbor's house. I realized that I forgot to pick up some yogurt. I decide to walk back to the weird-ass mini grocery in the center of the village, despite the fact that the small coffee-bar on the far side will be brimming with farmers at this time of the day, I make my way to the store. I pull my shoulders back and hold my head-high; I don't care that the farmers are probably already there, on break having a coffee. I decide to pick up a few kilos of haricots verts (Green beans) as well. I pick the very best and then help myself to the scale, weighing them with confidence. I sort of nod my head and smile at the farmers who are watching my every move from the strange bar on the other side. What the hell, it gives them something to talk about.

I passed back through the garden and walk by the mini-van. It still amazes me that I tower over it, but as I walk past it this time I kind of run my hand along the top of it affectionately, as I head toward our tiny home.

I noticed several new Rose Tremiere had bloomed last night, mostly hot-pink, they are starting to bloom more frequently again. I pick up a bunch of figs that have fallen from the tree above. I reach for the key to the house which is stored in the mailbox, of course and I don't even have a second thought about buglers or Medco-locks.

I look over to the laundry line where the bathroom rug's hanging out to dry; everything is as it should be. Oh it's 11am. I better get-over to the gas station before they close and also I wanted to pick up a few new bathing suit bottoms, I might even find a top to go with it and have a complete bikini, but really- who needs a top? I also notice that it seems to be getting sunny outside and I think about going back to the beach to sunbath, didn't want to miss an opportunity to hit the beach. My tan had mostly faded during the winter and I wanted to get a good base going again.

As I reach into the mailbox for our house key I notice that there was something else inside; a letter from my friend Mary, stuffed inside a CNBC envelope. Wow, CNBC. It almost made me snap out of my dream-state, my relaxed demeanor stiffened a bit. I thought how it looked oddly and vaguely familiar, the logo that is. I have this wave of memories from my past life, New York and subways and Sunday brunches. The flashback gets more vivid; I seem to remember running down the hallway to deliver a tape to playback with mere-seconds to air... working in the insanity of live news, as if it were some past life experience. The letter, unopened, seems to transport me through time and space. I have a rush of adrenaline as I remember how heavy and tense the atmosphere gets just moments before we go on the air. But I am so relaxed here. So calm, so slow, I am anything but the hyped-up Judy I was such a short time ago.

I suddenly have the sensation that I've been put into a witness protection program; complete with a new identity, new love, new language, and new toilettes. Not to mention tanned boobs, skinny ass-jeans and a reasonably impeccable French accent.

The new customs and challenges have become daily rituals. I have even become accustomed to the way everyone says my name here. Here, I simply am Judith, Szhooodiete. The mere fact that – having a different name isn't odd anymore... is weird unto itself. I am not even the tiniest bit uneasy anymore, rather I feel comforted by it. I think if I was completely honest I'd say I quite like it now.

I don't want to brag but I do know how to stick shift and I can read labels at the grocery store. I also know how to smell-cheese, (Sort-of) I just prefer not to. I like to see the gypsy children when I exit the store, as long as they keep their distance. I am probably most proud to acknowledge that I am tanned-all over, yet completely rash-free.

Finally, this Island is my home now. I really belong here. A few weeks ago, I woke up one morning and I realized I had dreamt in French. My entire dream took place in vivid, articulate, fabulous French and I awoke knowing that the language had seeped into my soul. I felt like it was such a breakthrough. The language has nested into my consciousness, my subconscious, and so deep into my being, that it is now part of me. I stopped translating somewhere along the line. No delay while I figured out what something meant. I just bypassed all of that. I believe it's a quantum leap of sorts, when you start to think in another language.

I've become an ex-New Yorker. I am a woman who not only lives in France now, but thinks of l'île d'Oléron as my place on the planet, my home.

Now I know my way around town and I know when the gas station is open and closed and although I am back to driving the mini-van again, I am in control of the stick shift, not the other way around. I hope never to have to push it, ever again, but if it comes to pass, I know I can handle it. I won't dare say I've become a master of the French driving experience; although I have managed to keep the mini-van in one piece, (Bravo!) and I can exit a 'rond-point' in under twelve minutes.

I know many people in town and exactly how many times to kiss them hello and goodbye! I have become the master of the art of café sitting. I can even sit through a three-four hour meal without getting up to stretch my legs.

And just like I began to dream in French, I began to live in French. Quite the revelation; I live in France, this Island is my Island. I do not know when I stopped making observations as a foreigner, maybe I never really did. But there was a transition of sorts, that happened somewhere in my life and time here. Maybe it was when I said "I do." I do accept my life here and will enjoy every moment of it. Sometimes I still wonder will I wake up from this dream, am I watching a movie and the lights in the theater will suddenly turn on. Which life is a dream the one here or the one there- or can they both exist? Do they just exist inside of me? I still go to the beach and look longingly at the other side of the Atlantic from time to time, but my feet are happily grounded in the sand at Verte Bois, our special beach in Le Deux.

How can NBC and New York City and hailing a taxi seem so distant when I did that for almost ten years? As I stand in the garden, the new flowers seem to break out from their buds and push fresh color into the almost-summer breeze. I stare at the letter from my friend Mary and touch the raised ink of the logo and I stare. I know I want to pour a nice glass of wine and take my time to read this note from home. I sure wouldn't want to rush through that.

I always wanted to embrace another culture another country and I did it. I mean, I wanted to delve in and taste every morsel of it, not as a tourist but feel like a real local. I love the mini-cars, mini-streets, t-tiny houses, with beautiful people, (Some with hoods, some without) and stunning crazy flowers that rise from every crevice and crack in the earth. I am truly, madly and deeply in love with this tiny village of fifty. And I'm even finally at ease with the fact that I am what the farmer's will talk about, so what? I adore every inch, or centimeter of my life here, and especially all the differences. The stillness at night, the space and peace – it allows and encourages my growth. And I am so grateful that I had the chance and the nerve to come here. I am not having a lucid dream I'm just living out my polar-opposite life.

I will say that this has been the most mind-expanding experience of anything else I have ever known or done. I'm so glad I packed my bags and headed here instead of Fire Island. I like being forced out of my comfort zone, and from all that I know. Don't get me wrong, I miss Manhattan and all the people in it. But from where I sit, which happens to be on an odd shaped toilet, it doesn't get much better than this.

Special Thanks

To my dear friends from L'île d'Oléron who welcomed me with open arms. Thank you for making my time with you one of the best chapters of my life.
And to my friends and family on this side of The Atlantic, who always love and support me no matter where I live, thank you from the bottom of my heart.